I0115712

Autism Gentle Parenting

Transformative Techniques Through Positive Discipline

Jennifer Meller

Copyright © 2023 by Jennifer Meller

All rights reserved.

No portion of this book may be reproduced in any form without written permission from the publisher or author, except as permitted by U.S. copyright law.

Contents

Chapter One

Introduction

Dear cherished reader,

Firstly, let me extend my heartfelt gratitude to you for picking up this book. It tells me you're on a profound journey, one filled with love, hope, challenges, and an unwavering desire to understand and nurture your child in the most respectful and compassionate way.

Navigating the world of autism can often feel like treading an intricate dance—one where every step, no matter how cautious, can lead to uncertainty. I know, because, like many of you, I've been there. Each tear shed, every moment of doubt, the silent wishes whispered into the night, hoping for guidance—these are all part of a narrative that many parents of autistic children can resonate with.

The essence of gentle parenting, especially tailored for autistic children, is not a one-size-fits-all strategy. Instead, it's a heartfelt commitment, a daily pledge to walk alongside our children, to see the world through their eyes, and to cultivate an environment where they can thrive as their authentic selves.

In "Autism Gentle Parenting: Transformative Techniques Through Positive Discipline", I aim to share insights and techniques that prioritize love, connection, understanding, and positive discipline. These are not mere tactics. They are a culmination of years of experience, research, and interactions with countless families like yours and mine.

Throughout this book, I invite you to embrace vulnerability, celebrate small victories, and be open to transformation. Remember, this isn't just about parenting. It's about forging a bond, built on trust and mutual respect, that stands the test of time.

So, as you turn the pages, I hope you find answers, solace, and most importantly, the affirmation that you are not alone on this journey. Together, hand in hand, with our children leading the way, we'll discover a world where love truly does conquer all.

With warmth and gratitude,
Jennifer Meller

Chapter Two

The Heart of Autism and Gentle Parenting

"Children with autism are not 'broken' or 'damaged'; they simply view the world through a different lens." - Anonymous

The journey you're embarking upon in these pages is not just about facts and figures, strategies or techniques—it's a deep dive into the vibrant world of autistic individuals, who, in their unique ways, offer us new perspectives on life, love, and understanding. As you pore over this chapter, I invite you to approach it with an open heart and mind, ready to challenge any preconceived notions and embrace the beauty of neurodiversity.

Understanding Autism

The term 'autism' might conjure up a variety of images and thoughts. For some, it could be a silent child engrossed in their world, while for others, it might be someone exceptionally talented in a particular domain. And yet, for many, it remains a mystery. Let's delve into understanding this vast spectrum.

What is Autism?

Autism, often referred to as Autism Spectrum Disorder (ASD), is a complex, multifaceted neurodevelopmental condition. At its core:

- It impacts how an individual perceives, interacts with, and understands their environment and those around them.

- Autism encompasses a spectrum, meaning it manifests differently in everyone. No two autistic individuals will have the exact same experiences or challenges.

- It's essential to understand that autism isn't a disease or something that needs 'fixing'. It's simply a different neurological construct.

Common Myths Debunked

Over the years, many myths surrounding autism have taken root, often causing misinformation and misunderstandings. Let's address a few of them:

- **"All autistic individuals are savants."** While some may have exceptional talents, it's a stereotype to believe all do.

- **"Autistic people lack emotions or empathy."** In reality, many autistic individuals feel emotions deeply; they might just express or process them differently.

- **"Autism is caused by vaccines."** Science has conclusively disproved this myth. Vaccines are essential and safe.

Embracing Neurodiversity

Neurodiversity is a beautiful concept that recognizes and celebrates the diverse ways our brains function. Embracing it means:

- Understanding that there's no 'normal' or 'right' way for the brain to work. Every individual offers a unique lens through which to view the world.

- Valuing the strengths and challenges that come with being neurodiverse.

- Advocating for acceptance, support, and understanding, rather than trying to fit everyone into a preconceived mold.

As we journey deeper into the heart of autism and gentle parenting, remember that this path is as much about understanding as it is about love. It's about seeing the world through a different lens and cherishing the vibrant hues it brings to our lives.

***

The Principles of Gentle Parenting

As you journey through these pages, I want to share with you a philosophy of parenting that goes beyond just managing behaviors. This approach is a beacon of love, understanding, and mutual respect. It's called 'gentle parenting,' and its foundation lies not in authority and discipline, but in connection, understanding, and patience. Let's delve deeper into this heart-centered approach together.

Connection over Correction

In traditional parenting, there's often an emphasis on "correcting" behavior, ensuring compliance, and establishing authority. While these methods might yield temporary compliance, they often miss the heart of what our children are trying to communicate.

In gentle parenting, the mantra is simple yet profound:

- Prioritize building a bond with your child, understanding their needs, emotions, and the reasons behind their actions.

- Recognize that behaviors are often just the tip of the iceberg. Underneath, there might be unmet needs, feelings of being overwhelmed, or simple developmental stages.

- By valuing connection over correction, we open doors to genuine understanding, deeper relationships, and lasting positive behaviors.

Empathy-driven Responses

Empathy is the ability to understand and share the feelings of another. As parents, our empathetic responses can be the bridge to our child's heart.

- Every cry, every tantrum, every silent moment has an emotion behind it. Instead of asking, "How can I fix this?" ask, "How might they be feeling?"

- By responding with empathy, we validate our children's feelings, making them feel seen, heard, and understood.

- Over time, these responses build trust, reduce power struggles, and foster emotional intelligence.

Importance of Being Present

In today's fast-paced world, one of the most precious gifts we can give our children is our undivided attention. Being present isn't just about being physically there; it's about immersing ourselves wholly in moments with our child.

- It's the small moments: the shared giggles, the bedtime stories, the curious questions, and the walks in the park.

- Being present means actively listening, engaging with genuine interest, and putting aside distractions.

- Through these moments, we communicate a powerful message: "You matter. You are valued. You are loved."

As we embrace the principles of gentle parenting, we're not just raising children. We're cultivating relationships, building trust, and nurturing the next generation with love and understanding. Remember, dear reader, it's not about being a perfect parent but a present, connected, and empathetic one.

***

Marrying Autism Understanding with Gentle Techniques

As our journey through the intricacies of autism and gentle parenting intertwines, there's a beautiful alignment waiting to be discovered. Each autistic child, with their unique blend of challenges and strengths, offers a canvas upon which gentle techniques can paint a masterpiece of love, understanding, and growth. Let us delve into the art of marrying our understanding of autism with the heart-centered approach of gentle parenting.

Recognizing Unique Challenges

Every child is a universe unto themselves, and when it comes to children on the autism spectrum, this individuality shines even brighter.

- Dive deep into observation. Notice the sensory sensitivities, the patterns of behavior, and the ways in which they communicate.

- Understand that while there might be common threads among autistic individuals, your child's experience is uniquely theirs. Their challenges, though sometimes shared with others, require personalized understanding and approach.

- This recognition is the foundation upon which our gentle techniques can be tailored.

Tailoring Gentle Methods

With a clear understanding of the unique challenges, we can adapt our gentle parenting toolbox to meet our child's specific needs.

- Perhaps, for your child, a soft-spoken reassurance works wonders during overwhelming moments, while for another, a silent hug speaks volumes.

- It could be about creating sensory-friendly environments, understanding non-verbal cues, or simply discovering what makes them feel safe and loved.

- This tailoring isn't about changing the essence of gentle parenting but about molding it in a way that resonates with your child's world.

Celebrating Small Victories

In this journey, every step forward, no matter how tiny, is a victory worth celebrating.

- The first time they communicate a need, even if it's through a gesture, is monumental.

- The moments when they find solace in your embrace during a meltdown, the instances when they achieve something they've been working on—these are the milestones that warm our hearts.

- Celebrating these small victories not only boosts their confidence but also strengthens our resolve and belief in the power of gentle, understanding parenting.

As we marry our understanding of autism with gentle techniques, we are sowing seeds of love, patience, and acceptance. We are honoring our children's individuality while equipping ourselves with the tools to guide, support, and celebrate them in the most heartfelt way. Always remember, in this journey, you're not walking alone. Together, through these pages, we walk hand in hand, cherishing every step.

***

Why Positive Discipline?

As we navigate the landscape of parenting, one term that has steadily emerged at the forefront is "Positive Discipline." You might wonder, amidst a myriad of parenting techniques, why place our emphasis here? Let's embark on this segment together, as we uncover the transformative power of Positive Discipline, especially in the world of autism and gentle parenting.

Moving Beyond Punishment

Throughout history, discipline has often synonymous with punishment. The belief was straightforward - correct a behavior through punitive measures, and it won't reoccur. But, as we've evolved in our understanding:

- We've realized that punishment often addresses the symptom, not the root cause.

- Rather than instilling understanding, punishment can breed fear, resentment, and a fractured parent-child relationship.

- Positive Discipline shifts this paradigm. It moves us from punitive responses to collaborative problem-solving, focusing on solutions and mutual respect.

Fostering Intrinsic Motivation

One of the most profound gifts we can bestow upon our children is the drive to do things not because they're told to, but because they understand and want to.

- Intrinsic motivation isn't built overnight. It's cultivated when children feel involved, valued, and understood.

- Positive Discipline doesn't rely on external rewards or threats. Instead, it nurtures a child's internal compass, fostering a genuine understanding of actions and consequences.

Building Resilience and Self-Regulation

Life, as we know, is a tapestry of ups and downs. Resilience is what enables us to bounce back from setbacks, and self-regulation helps us manage our emotions effectively.

- Positive Discipline equips children with the tools to face challenges, learn from mistakes, and emerge stronger.

- By understanding consequences in a safe and supportive environment, they develop the ability to self-regulate, to pause and reflect before reacting.

As we dive deeper into the embrace of Positive Discipline, it's not just about a method-ology. It's a heart-centered approach, one that respects our children, values their input, and believes in their potential. It reminds us that discipline isn't about control, but about guidance; not about demands, but understanding. As we move forward, remember, that every child has a wellspring of potential, and with Positive Discipline, we're simply allowing it to flourish.

***

Setting the Stage for Success

In the theater of life, where each day is an act and every interaction a scene, the stage we set plays a pivotal role in the performance we deliver. Especially in the world of gentle parenting and understanding autism, it's crucial to prime ourselves, ensuring that we're in the best position to support our radiant stars – our children. Allow me to guide you through this preparative journey, as we set the stage for a performance brimming with love, understanding, and success.

Preparing Yourself Mentally

Embarking on this journey requires a mindset shift, one that's foundational to all the steps that follow:

- Understand that this path, like any other, will have its ebbs and flows. Equip yourself with knowledge, seek out resources, and lean into communities that share your goals.

- Recognize and acknowledge your emotions. It's okay to feel overwhelmed or uncertain at times. These feelings don't define your ability to parent; they make you human.

- Mental preparation is about cultivating an open heart, a curious mind, and the belief that change and growth are always within reach.

Embracing Patience and Persistence

Rome wasn't built in a day, and neither is the intricate process of gentle parenting.

- Understand that every child, especially those on the autism spectrum, has a unique timeline of growth. Rushing them or setting unrealistic expectations can hamper progress.

- Remember that setbacks are natural. They're not roadblocks but stepping stones. With persistence and unwavering support, what seems challenging today might become second nature tomorrow.

Celebrating Progress, Not Perfection

In our quest for success, it's easy to become fixated on perfection. But the beauty of life lies in the journey, not just the destination.

- Rejoice in the little moments, the tiny steps forward. Maybe today, there was one less meltdown, or perhaps there was a new word spoken or gesture made.

- Celebrate yourself too. For every moment of patience, for every loving gesture, for being the anchor in your child's life.

- Remember, it's the consistent progress, the journey of growth, that truly matters. Perfection is not the goal; a loving, understanding relationship is.

As we set the stage for success, I want you to know that you're not just building a framework for your child but also for yourself. You're evolving, learning, and growing. And as you do, you're crafting a world where love reigns supreme, where challenges become stepping stones, and where every day is a testament to the boundless power of understanding and connection.

Chapter Three

Laying the Foundations for Positive Discipline

"Do not train children to learn by force and harshness, but direct them to it by what amuses their minds." - Plato

In the gentle dance of parenting, every step, every nuance, and every turn counts. Especially when navigating the world of children with autism, the rhythm we set and the foundations we lay have profound implications. In this chapter, we'll immerse ourselves in the core essence of Positive Discipline – a philosophy that stands as a beacon of connection, understanding, and mutual respect.

Picture for a moment a skyscraper, standing tall against the skyline. What we often admire is its majestic height, the beautiful architecture, or the panoramic views from the top. However, what keeps it standing tall, weathering storms and time, is its foundation. Similarly, the beauty of Positive Discipline lies not just in its techniques but in the solid foundations upon which they are built.

Positive Discipline, at its heart, is about creating a space where children feel valued, understood, and capable. It's a shift from the traditional paradigms of rewards and punishments to a realm where mistakes are opportunities to learn, where challenges are met with understanding, and where the focus is on solutions, not blame.

As we embark on this chapter, we will explore:

- The philosophical underpinnings of Positive Discipline and its emphasis on mutual respect and community.

- How this approach empowers children, fostering a sense of belonging and significance.

- The pivotal role of connection in guiding behavior, and how it trumps correction every time.

- Techniques to shift from a mindset of control to one of cooperation, making discipline a collaborative effort.

- The transformative power of seeing misbehavior as a message, a call for help, rather than an act of defiance.

While the tenets of Positive Discipline are universally beneficial, when applied with an understanding of autism, they take on an added layer of significance. The nuances, the challenges, and the unique strengths of children on the spectrum require a gentle hand, a listening ear, and a heart full of patience. Through Positive Discipline, we find the tools, the understanding, and the philosophy to create an environment where every child, irrespective of their neurotype, feels understood, capable, and above all, loved.

Let's lay these foundations together, brick by brick, belief by belief. And as we do, let's remember that every house, no matter how grand, stands tall and proud because of the foundation it's built upon.

***

Understanding Behavior as Communication

In the symphony of life, not all notes are vocalized. Some of the most profound melodies are silent, resonating in the realm of behaviors, actions, and gestures. This is especially true when we dive into the world of children with autism. Their behaviors, often misunderstood or misinterpreted, are rich tapestries of messages waiting to be deciphered.

Decoding Non-Verbal Cues

Much like an artist expresses through their canvas, children, especially those on the autism spectrum, often convey their emotions, needs, and feelings without words.

- A flapping hand might be a sign of excitement or overwhelm.

- Avoiding eye contact doesn't necessarily denote disinterest; it could be a way of processing information or managing sensory input.

- It's essential to observe, listen with our hearts, and become fluent in this silent language, for it opens the doors to deeper understanding and connection.

Recognizing Triggers and Stressors

Imagine walking a mile in their shoes. The world can be an overwhelming place, filled with sensory stimuli that might seem innocuous to us but can be intense for them.

- A buzzing light, a scratchy tag on a shirt, or a room full of chatter can trigger discomfort or distress.

- Recognizing these triggers, and understanding what might escalate a situation, or what brings solace, is pivotal. It's the first step in ensuring their environment is nurturing and supportive.

Embracing Proactive Strategies

Forewarned is forearmed. When we can anticipate potential challenges or understand the underlying messages of certain behaviors, we can be proactive rather than reactive.

- Create safe spaces where they can retreat to when feeling overwhelmed.

- Use visual aids or other tools to help them express their needs or emotions.

- Cultivate routines and predictability, providing them with a sense of security and structure.

Beloved reader, as we navigate this segment, I want to emphasize the transformative power of understanding behavior as a communication. It's about looking beyond the surface, delving deeper into the 'why' behind the 'what'. It's about replacing judgments with curiosity, and frustrations with empathy. In doing so, we not only pave the way for effective positive discipline but also forge bonds of trust, respect, and deep connection.

***

Setting Up a Nurturing Environment

Imagine, for a moment, stepping into a space that feels like a warm embrace. A place where every corner whispers reassurance, where every element seems tailored to cater to your comforts, and where you feel an innate sense of belonging. Such is the magic of a nurturing environment, especially vital for our children on the autism spectrum.

Routines and predictability serve as anchors in the vast ocean of life's unpredictability. Just like we find solace in our morning cup of coffee or the familiar tune of a beloved song, children with autism often thrive when there's a predictable rhythm to their day. This consistency doesn't stifle; instead, it provides a safe framework within which they can explore, learn, and grow.

But the environment isn't just about time; it's also about space. A sensory-friendly space is akin to a sanctuary for children with autism. Reducing overwhelming stimuli, choosing calming colors, or even incorporating soft textures can make a world of difference. It's about understanding their unique sensory needs and crafting spaces that respect and cater to them.

Now, amidst all this comfort, there's also a profound strength in fostering independence. It's like teaching them to dance in the rain, instead of just providing an umbrella. Encouraging them to perform tasks on their own, be it tying their shoelaces or setting the table, not only equips them with skills but also instills a sense of achievement and self-worth.

Here are some detailed guidelines and ideas to help you create such an environment:

    1. **Embrace Consistency:** Children with autism often thrive in predictable envi-

ronments. Establish and maintain daily routines, such as consistent meal, bath, and bedtime schedules. The more predictable their world is, the safer and more secure they feel.

2. **Sensory Considerations:**

   ○ **Visual:** Soft, muted colors on walls can be calming. Consider installing dimmable lights so you can adjust the brightness based on the child's comfort.

   ○ **Auditory:** Some children might be hypersensitive to noises. White noise machines, soft instrumental music, or noise-canceling headphones can be useful.

   ○ **Tactile:** Use soft fabrics for bedding and clothing. Weighted blankets can provide comfort. Avoid tags in clothing or rough textures that might irritate.

   ○ **Spatial:** Create designated spaces for different activities. A quiet reading corner, a play area, and a space for relaxation can help a child transition between activities more smoothly.

3. **Clear Organization:** Use labeled bins and shelves so that everything has a designated spot. This helps in reducing anxiety associated with unpredictability.

4. **Visual Supports:** Visual cues, like picture schedules, charts, or labels, can assist a child in understanding what's expected. For non-verbal children, picture communication systems can be invaluable.

5. **Safety First:** Secure furniture to walls, avoid sharp corners, and use gates or locks if needed. For children prone to wandering, alarms on doors or tracking devices can provide an added layer of safety.

6. **Flexible Spaces:** Use movable furniture or room dividers to adjust the space based on the child's needs. This allows for versatility—maybe today it's a playroom, but tomorrow it becomes a quiet reading area.

7. **Empower with Choice:** Create areas where your child can make decisions, such as a toy shelf they can access or a snack bin with healthy choices.

8. **Incorporate Nature:** Natural elements have a calming effect. Consider introducing houseplants, a fish tank, or a small indoor fountain. If possible, set up a safe outdoor space for them to explore.

9. **Interactive Zones:** Designate areas where children can engage in sensory play, like sand or water tables, tactile wall panels, or DIY sensory boards.

10. **Respectful Boundaries:** Just as there are spaces for interaction and activity, there should be clear zones where the child can retreat to and be alone when feeling overwhelmed.

11. **Continual Learning and Adapting:** Remember that every child is unique. What works for one might not work for another. Continually observe, adapt, and modify the environment based on your child's responses and changing needs.

Creating a nurturing environment is as much about the physical space as it is about the emotional atmosphere. Approach the process with patience, empathy, and an open heart. Listen to your child's cues—they often have the best insights into what makes them feel most comfortable and secure.

***

Creating Effective Boundaries

In the vast tapestry of parenting, especially when navigating the unique landscapes of autism, the art of setting boundaries can seem both daunting and absolutely essential. Just as the banks of a river guide its flow, giving it direction and purpose, boundaries in the lives of our children serve a similar purpose.

Boundaries matter, not just because they instill discipline, but because they offer a sense of safety. Much like how a toddler finds comfort in the snug embrace of their crib, knowing its boundaries, our children, even with their boundless energy and curiosity, find reassurance in the predictability that well-set boundaries provide. They help children understand the world around them, making it a little less overwhelming.

Yet, the magic lies not just in setting these boundaries but in ensuring they are clear and consistent. Imagine trying to play a game where the rules keep changing; it'd be frustrating, wouldn't it? In the same vein, when our boundaries shift often, it can create a sense of instability for our child. Consistency offers them a playbook to life's many games, a guide they can rely on.

However, as you well know, boundaries aren't walls or barriers; they are guides. And guides, my dear reader, are most effective when they're reinforced with kindness. While it's important to be firm, it's equally crucial to pair firmness with understanding and compassion. Instead of a stern "no", imagine the transformative power of a "no, because..." followed by a loving explanation.

In the realm of autism gentle parenting, setting boundaries doesn't mean stifling or suppressing. It means providing our children with a framework where they can safely explore, learn, and grow. It's about striking a balance between their need for independence and our instinct to protect, guide, and nurture.

As you journey through this chapter, I invite you to envision boundaries not as restrictions, but as loving arms guiding your child through the maze of life, arms that are steadfast yet gentle, protective yet empowering.

Creating effective boundaries involves a blend of understanding, consistency, and empathy, especially when working with children on the autism spectrum. Here are some practical examples to illuminate this concept further:

1. **Screen Time Limitation:**

   ○ *Example:* If your child enjoys watching videos or playing on a tablet, you might set a clear boundary of one hour of screen time after homework or chores are done.

○ *The Kind Explanation:* "We have an hour for videos because after that, it's good for our eyes and brain to rest and do something different."

2. Safe Spaces in the Home:

○ *Example:* Maybe there's a room or section of the house that's off-limits because of potential hazards, like a workshop.

○ *The Kind Explanation:* "That area is just for grown-ups because it has tools and things that might be unsafe for little hands."

3. Behavioral Expectations in Public Spaces:

○ *Example:* If you're going to a store, set a boundary like staying close to the shopping cart or holding a parent's hand.

○ *The Kind Explanation:* "When we're in busy places, it's important to stay close so we can keep each other safe and not get lost."

4. Setting Dietary Boundaries:

○ *Example:* Maybe sugary snacks are limited to once a day.

○ *The Kind Explanation:* "Sweets are tasty, but too much can make our tummies hurt and our teeth unhappy. Let's save the candy for after dinner!"

5. Social Interactions:

○ *Example:* It's okay to say "no" if someone wants to play with their special toy.

○ *The Kind Explanation:* "It's okay to have things that are just yours. If you don't want to share your special toy today, you can say 'no thank you'."

6. Handling Emotions:

○ *Example:* It's okay to feel angry, but it's not okay to hit.

○ *The Kind Explanation:* "I understand you're upset, and that's okay. Let's find a way to express our anger without hurting others."

7. **Bedtime Routine:**

- *Example:* After the bedtime story, it's time for lights out.

- *The Kind Explanation:* "Once our story is done, it's time for our bodies and minds to rest so we can be fresh and energetic tomorrow."

8. **Personal Space and Boundaries:**

- *Example:* It's important to knock before entering someone's room.

- *The Kind Explanation:* "Just like you have your own special space, others do too. We knock to show respect and to ask if we can come in."

9. **Limiting Stimuli:**

- *Example:* When feeling overwhelmed in a busy setting, use noise-cancelling headphones.

- *The Kind Explanation:* "Sometimes, places can be really noisy. These head-phones can help make things quieter for you."

10. **Participation in Chores:**

- *Example:* Setting a clear expectation like putting away toys after playing.

- *The Kind Explanation:* "After we play, we put our toys back so our space is tidy, and we can find them easily next time."

The key to effective boundaries, especially for children with autism, lies in consistency, clarity, and ensuring that the boundary serves a purpose that benefits the child. When these principles are combined with empathy and understanding, boundaries become tools for empowerment and growth rather than mere restrictions.

Building a Trusting Relationship

Navigating the intricate paths of parenting can often feel like treading a tightrope, balancing between guidance and freedom, protection and independence. But at the heart of this delicate dance lies a foundational element that makes the journey smoother and more rewarding: trust. Building a trusting relationship with your child, especially one with autism, is akin to creating a sturdy bridge over life's turbulent rivers, providing safe passage for both of you.

Being a Safe Space for Your Child

One of the most heartwarming sights in nature is that of a fledgling taking refuge under the protective wings of its parent. Our children, regardless of where they fall on the spectrum, crave this safety. They need to know that with us, they are safe not just physically, but emotionally and mentally. This means being there for them without judgment, ready to embrace their uniqueness, their fears, joys, and everything in between. When they melt down or grapple with challenges that seem insurmountable, our role isn't to fix them but to stand beside them, offering a harbor in life's storm.

Cultivating Open Communication

Imagine a garden, verdant and full of life. Just as water is vital for its growth, open communication nourishes the relationship between parent and child. Encourage them to express themselves, even if it's not in words. Sometimes, a drawing, a gesture, or a simple action can convey volumes. And when they do communicate, listen with your heart as much as your ears. Celebrate their efforts and reassure them that their voice, no matter how it emerges, is valid and valued.

Prioritizing Connection Over Control

At times, as parents, it's easy to slip into a pattern of seeking control, especially when we're driven by a genuine desire to protect our children. But the true essence of parenting, especially gentle parenting, is connection. When faced with challenges, instead of asking, "How can I manage this situation?" consider, "How can I connect with my child right now?" This shift in perspective can transform moments of tension into opportunities for bonding.

As you embark on this journey of building trust, remember that every child is a universe unto themselves, vast and full of potential. Your role, as their guide and ally, is to walk alongside them, illuminating their path with understanding, patience, and an unwavering belief in their abilities. Through genuine connection and open communication, you'll find that the trust you cultivate will become the strongest pillar in your parenting journey.

Building a trusting relationship with your child, especially if they're on the autism spectrum, requires patience, understanding, and consistency. Here are some expanded insights and examples:

Being Present and Attentive

Insight: Being present means giving your full attention when your child is communicating with you. This builds trust as they feel heard and valued.

Example: If your child is trying to share a story or express how they feel, even if it's in a non-verbal manner, make sure to put away distractions like your phone or turn off the TV. This way, you can focus fully on what they're conveying.

Being Predictable

Insight: Children, especially those with autism, often find comfort in routines and predictability. Being consistent in your actions and responses provides a sense of stability.

Example: If you've established a bedtime routine, sticking to it daily can be reassuring for your child. This consistency can help build trust as they know what to expect.

Validating Feelings

Insight: Every emotion your child feels is valid. By acknowledging and validating these feelings, you're building a foundation of trust.

Example: If your child is frustrated because they can't express themselves clearly, instead of dismissing their feelings, you could say, "I can see you're feeling upset. I'm here to help and listen."

Apologizing When Necessary

Insight: Everyone makes mistakes, including parents. Owning up to them and apologizing demonstrates to your child that you value their feelings and are accountable for your actions.

Example: If you mistakenly raise your voice or misunderstand your child's needs, a simple "I'm sorry, I made a mistake" can go a long way in mending trust.

Empowering Choices

Insight: By giving your child choices, even small ones, you're showing that you trust and value their decisions, which in turn encourages them to trust you.

Example: Instead of deciding on a weekend activity yourself, ask your child if they'd prefer a trip to the park or a day at the museum.

Quality Time Together

Insight: Spending quality time together fosters closeness and trust. This doesn't necessarily mean elaborate activities; it can be as simple as reading a book together or cooking a meal.

Example: Dedicate a 'family day' or 'special time' where you and your child engage in an activity they love. This dedicated time shows that they are a priority.

Maintain Privacy

Insight: As children grow, they begin to value their privacy more. Respecting this builds trust.

Example: If your child writes in a journal, ensure you never read it without their permission. Respecting their private space and thoughts reinforces the trust they have in you.

Transparency and Honesty

Insight: Children are more observant than we sometimes realize. Being transparent and honest, in age-appropriate ways, can help establish a foundation of trust.

Example: If there's a change in routine or a challenging situation ahead, discussing it openly with your child prepares them and reinforces the idea that you're a team.

Remember, building trust is a continuous process. It's the accumulation of countless little moments of understanding, patience, and love. As your child evolves, so will the ways in which you foster and nurture this trust.

***

Developing Emotional Literacy

In the grand tapestry of human interaction, emotions are the vibrant threads that weave our experiences together. They color our world, give depth to our memories, and guide our decisions. Yet, for many of us, understanding and managing these emotions – in ourselves and in others – can be a challenge. This is especially true for children, and even more so for those on the autism spectrum. That's where emotional literacy comes into play.

Encouraging Emotion Identification
Our emotions can often feel like a tumultuous sea, with waves of feelings crashing into one another, making it hard to distinguish one from the next. Teaching our children to identify these emotions is the first step in navigating these waters. Start by naming the emotions when they arise. For instance, when watching a movie, you might point out, "Look at that character. They seem sad because they lost their toy." Over time, this simple act of naming can help your child better recognize and articulate their feelings.

Validating Feelings Without Judgment
Imagine you're sharing a difficult experience, and someone dismisses your feelings or tells you how you should feel instead. It's hurtful and invalidating. Children feel the same way.

Every emotion your child experiences is valid, regardless of the cause. Instead of saying, "There's no reason to be upset over a toy," try, "I understand you're upset because you can't find your toy. Let's try to find it together." Such responses not only validate your child's feelings but also reinforce that you're there to support them.

Fostering Emotional Regulation Skills

While it's crucial to understand and validate emotions, it's equally important to equip our children with the tools to manage them. Emotional regulation isn't about suppressing feelings but navigating them in healthy ways. Teach your child deep breathing exercises when they're feeling overwhelmed, or create a "calm down" corner in your home stocked with soft blankets, favorite books, and sensory tools. By practicing these techniques during calm moments, they'll be better prepared to use them when emotions run high.

Developing emotional literacy in our children is akin to gifting them a compass for life's vast ocean of experiences. It won't always prevent the storms, but it provides them with the tools to navigate through them. As you embark on this journey alongside your child, remember that patience, understanding, and consistent practice are your best allies.

Chapter Four

Communication

Bridging the Gap with Empathy and Understanding

"Autism... offers a chance for us to glimpse an awe-filled vision of the world that might otherwise pass us by." - Dr. Colin Zimbleman

In a world teeming with languages, dialects, and a myriad of ways to express ourselves, communication remains a profound enigma. We've all experienced that pang of frustration when our words fall on deaf ears or are misconstrued entirely. For a child on the autism spectrum, this experience is magnified tenfold. They're often trapped in a dichotomy of desperately wanting to connect while grappling with an inherently unique way of processing the world. However, the beauty of communication is its adaptability, and its ability to evolve. This chapter aims to illuminate that path toward meaningful connection, driven by empathy and understanding.

Recognizing Non-verbal Cues

Many children with autism communicate more with actions than with words. Their behaviors, their movements, and even their silences carry messages waiting to be understood. Perhaps it's the way they avoid eye contact when overwhelmed or the specific stimming action they resort to when excited. By becoming attuned to these non-verbal cues, we can decipher a wealth of information. It's akin to learning a new language, one of profound depth and nuance.

The Power of Active Listening

While we're often keen to offer our insights or solutions, there's profound power in simply listening. Active listening isn't just about hearing words; it's about diving deep into the sentiments behind them. It's about validating feelings, asking open-ended questions, and ensuring the child feels truly heard. This form of listening is a gift of presence, one that paves the way for trust and understanding.

Embracing the Uniqueness of Their Voice

Every child on the autism spectrum has a unique voice and a distinctive way of expressing themselves. Some might find solace in drawing, others in music, and some in the rhythmic cadence of scripted dialogues. Celebrate these unique avenues of expression. They're not just communication tools; they're windows into their soul.

Empathy: The Heartbeat of Connection

If communication is the bridge, empathy is its foundation. To empathize is to step into their shoes, to feel their joys, their fears, and their frustrations. It's a journey of heart-to-heart connection, where words often take a back seat to feelings. When we approach communication with empathy, we're not just exchanging words; we're building bonds.

As you delve into this chapter, I invite you to see communication not just as an exchange of words but as an art. An art of connecting, of understanding, of building bridges across vast chasms of experiences. And at the heart of this art lies empathy, the golden thread that weaves us all together.

***

Decoding Non-Verbal Communication

Have you ever found yourself in a bustling foreign market, surrounded by unfamiliar sounds, sights, and languages? Amidst this cacophony, have you noticed the way the stall owner's eyes light up when they showcase their best products, or the slight tilt of a shopper's head as they haggle over prices? Without uttering a word in your native tongue, you've managed to communicate, negotiate, and understand using the universal language of body language.

Similarly, the realm of non-verbal communication, especially with children on the autism spectrum, is akin to navigating such a vibrant, wordless marketplace. Their expressions, gestures, and behaviors offer a wealth of insight into their inner world, and our challenge is to learn to 'speak' and 'understand' this silent language.

Recognizing Body Language Cues

Body language is a symphony of subtle cues. The fidgeting of fingers might indicate anxiety, while flapping hands could be a sign of excitement or overwhelm. A downturned head might suggest sadness, while a child retreating to a corner could mean they need a break. Just as a musician learns to recognize each note and its variations, we too can tune our senses to these cues, understanding their significance in the child's unique context.

The Power of Observation and Patience

The art of decoding non-verbal communication is not one mastered overnight. It requires observation, patience, and, above all, presence. Spend time simply observing your child in different settings: during play, during meals, or even during quiet moments. Like a detective piecing together clues, patterns will emerge, granting you deeper insights into their world. But remember, patience is key. It's a journey of discovery, one that evolves as your child grows and changes.

Using Tools and Aids to Facilitate Communication

In our quest to bridge the communication gap, we're not alone. Numerous tools, ranging from picture cards (PECS) to communication apps, can be invaluable allies. These aids can empower children, providing them with an avenue to express themselves when words might fail them. It's essential, however, to tailor these tools to your child's needs, ensuring they complement rather than override their unique communication style.

I wish to leave you with a thought. While the journey of decoding non-verbal communication might seem daunting, it's also profoundly rewarding. For in those silent exchanges, in those wordless moments, lies the essence of genuine connection, a bond that transcends language and touches the very soul.

Recognizing Body Language Cues

Example 1: **Eye Contact and Gaze**

When Sarah's son, Liam, who's on the autism spectrum, wants a specific toy that's out of his reach, he doesn't verbalize his desire. Instead, he focuses his gaze intently on the toy, occasionally glancing back at Sarah, silently urging her to understand his request. Over time, Sarah learned to discern the subtle difference between Liam's casual looking around and this pointed gaze, which indicates a particular interest or need.

Example 2: **Physical Distance**

Jake, a 10-year-old with ASD, tends to move closer to people he trusts and likes. When overwhelmed or anxious, he distances himself, often finding a quiet corner. His parents have come to understand that Jake's proximity isn't just about physical space; it's a direct reflection of his comfort level and emotional state.

The Power of Observation and Patience

Example 3: **Stimming Behaviors**

Mila noticed that her daughter, Ava, would often twirl her hair around her fingers when she was anxious. Initially, she thought it was just a harmless habit. However, by observing closely, Mila recognized a pattern: Ava's hair twirling increased during loud events or when surrounded by unfamiliar people. Recognizing this allowed Mila to proactively address Ava's anxiety before it escalated.

Example 4: **Mealtime Observations**

During meals, Ryan would often tap his fork on his plate repeatedly before eating. His parents initially dismissed it as a quirk. But with patience, they observed that this tapping increased when Ryan was served unfamiliar or disliked foods. The tapping was his non-verbal way of expressing unease or dissatisfaction.

Using Tools and Aids to Facilitate Communication

Example 5: **Picture Exchange Communication System (PECS)**

Ella, who is minimally verbal, carries a small binder with laminated cards depicting common items and emotions. When thirsty, she hands over the card with a glass of water illustrated on it. If she's feeling upset, she might show the card that depicts a sad face. This system has empowered Ella to communicate her needs and feelings effectively.

Example 6: **Digital Communication Apps**

Leo uses a tablet with a communication app that vocalizes phrases or words he selects. When he wants to go to the park, he navigates to the 'activities' section and selects the "park" icon. The tablet then verbalizes, "I want to go to the park," allowing Leo to communicate his desire audibly.

I hope these examples provide a tangible glimpse into the multifaceted world of non-verbal communication. Each child, with their unique personality and experiences, will have their distinct ways of expressing themselves. The key lies in observing, understanding, and responding with empathy and patience.

***

Encouraging Expressiveness

Have you ever listened to a piece of music that moved you deeply, even though there were no lyrics to dictate its story? Or perhaps you've been captivated by a painting, its colors and strokes evoking emotions words couldn't describe. Expression isn't always bound by language. For many, especially children on the autism spectrum, emotions, desires, and thoughts find a voice through alternative mediums.

Fostering a Non-Judgmental Space

Imagine, for a moment, being in a room where every move you make, every sound you emit, is scrutinized and evaluated. Intimidating, isn't it? Now, contrast that with a space where you're free to be, to explore, to express without the weight of judgment. That's the kind of environment we must strive to create for our children. Whether it's allowing them to wear mismatched socks or letting them hum their unique tunes, it's vital to give them the freedom to be authentically themselves. Such a space doesn't just encourage expressiveness; it nurtures the soul.

Empowering through Art, Music, and Play

Art isn't merely a pastime; it's a language. For children who might struggle with traditional communication, mediums like art, music, and play become their voice. Drawing can be a way to depict their day, feelings, or dreams. Drumming on a bongo might be their method of releasing frustration or showing joy. Play, with its unstructured beauty, can be a mirror to their inner world. By introducing them to various expressive outlets and tools - be it paintbrushes, instruments, or simple toys - we're handing them a microphone to their soul.

Celebrating Each Unique Mode of Expression

Every child is a universe of experiences, thoughts, and emotions. And each universe has its mode of communication. For some, it might be through meticulously built Lego structures. For others, it might be through interpretative dance or even the unique way they arrange their toys. As guardians and guides on their journey, it's our duty and privilege to recognize, honor, and celebrate these individual modes of expression.

In conclusion, expression is as varied as humanity itself. By fostering a safe, encouraging environment and providing the tools for artistic and playful exploration, we're not just aiding communication; we're validating our children's experiences and emotions. Always remember, in the grand tapestry of life, every form of expression, no matter how unconventional, adds color, texture, and beauty.

Here are some vivid examples that further illuminate the concept of **Encouraging Expressiveness**:

Example 1: **Mismatched Shoes**
Little Sophie wore two different shoes to school one day. Instead of pointing it out as an error, her teacher praised her unique style choice, asking if it was a new trend. Sophie beamed with pride, feeling accepted and encouraged to be herself.

Example 2: **Unique Sounds**
Ethan often communicated his excitement through a series of high-pitched squeals. While it drew attention in public places, his parents learned to respond by echoing his excitement, validating his feelings, rather than shushing him to conform to public expectations.

Empowering through Art, Music, and Play

Example 3: **Story Through Painting**
Maria, non-verbal and on the spectrum, created a series of watercolor paintings. Each painting depicted a scene from her day: a sunny park, a table spread with her favorite

snacks, and a dark cloud that symbolized her anxiety during a dentist visit. These paintings became her diary, her way of sharing her day with her family.

Example 4: **Music as Emotion**

Dylan struggled to express complex feelings verbally. But given a set of bongos, he would beat out rhythms that reflected his emotions. Quick, loud beats when he was upset or agitated, and slow, rhythmic beats when he was calm and content. Over time, his family began to understand his musical language.

Example 5: **Building Stories with Toys**

Jasmine would often line up her action figures in intricate patterns. Upon closer observation, her mother realized these figures were recreating scenarios, some from her day and some from her vivid imagination. A superhero standing guard by a sleeping figure symbolized her dad watching over her at night.

Celebrating Each Unique Mode of Expression

Example 6: **Dance as Expression**

Every evening, Alex would perform a 'dance of his day'. A series of jumps and twirls signified a good day, while slow, dragging steps showed he had a tough one. His family soon started joining in, creating a shared, expressive dance ritual.

Example 7: **Puzzle Messages**

Ben loved puzzles. One day, after a trip to the zoo, he assembled his puzzles to form the animals he'd seen that day, using them to recount his experience. His parents started getting him puzzles that represented various events and activities, allowing Ben to "talk" about his day.

As we witness and understand these examples, it becomes clear that when it comes to expression, there's no 'right' or 'wrong'. Each individual, especially a child with autism, has their unique language. It's our privilege and responsibility to listen, understand, and celebrate it.

***

Active Listening Techniques

In our bustling, fast-paced world, genuine listening has become a rare skill. Yet, for those of us blessed with children on the autism spectrum, mastering the art of active listening can unlock a treasure trove of understanding and connection. Let me share with you the intricacies of this beautiful craft.

Going Beyond Spoken Words

Have you ever noticed how sometimes, a mere look or gesture from someone can convey more than a thousand words? For many children, especially those on the spectrum, their richest communication might not always be verbal. It might be the slight flinch when they hear a loud noise, the fluttering of their eyelashes when they're content, or the way they clasp their favorite toy when they're anxious. As caregivers and parents, it's crucial to tune into these silent symphonies, for they often hold the key to understanding their inner worlds.

Example: When Luke's mother noticed he'd often tap his fingers rapidly against his thigh before having a meltdown, she realized it was his way of signaling overwhelming stress. Recognizing this cue allowed her to intervene with calming techniques before his distress escalated.

The Art of Pausing and Reflecting

In our eagerness to help, we often jump into solutions or responses too quickly. However, there's immense power in pausing, allowing a moment of silence, and then reflecting. This space can be the breathing room your child needs to process their feelings and thoughts, and it can also give you the clarity to respond most effectively.

Example: When Mia shared her distress about a change in school routine, instead of offering immediate solutions, her dad simply said, "It sounds like that change was really hard for you." This pause and reflection gave Mia the space to further express her feelings.

Validating and Echoing to Show Understanding

Validation doesn't necessarily mean agreement, but it does mean acknowledgment. It's the act of saying, "I see you. I hear you." Echoing, or repeating back a version of what's been shared, can be a powerful tool to show your child that you truly understand their perspective.

Example: When Aiden expressed, "I don't like loud places, they hurt," his mother responded with, "So, the loud noises feel painful to you." This validation and echoing reassured Aiden that his feelings were recognized and valued.

In closing, active listening is more than just hearing words. It's an immersion, a deep dive into the world of another, feeling with them, and understanding from their perspective. When you embrace this skill, you're not just bettering communication; you're building bridges of empathy and trust.

Let's delve deeper into the realm of **Active Listening Techniques** with our focus on those invaluable strategies:

Going Beyond Spoken Words

Intuitive Observations:
Zara seldom spoke about her feelings. But her mother noticed that whenever she was overwhelmed, she'd retreat to a corner and start humming. This humming was Zara's way of self-soothing. By recognizing this non-verbal cue, her mother could gently intervene, offering comfort or a break from the current activity.

Subtle Expressions:
Connor's eyes always darted to the door whenever guests arrived, signaling his discomfort with new entrants into his space. Recognizing this, his parents began preparing him in advance for any visitors, ensuring a smoother transition.

The Art of Pausing and Reflecting

Giving Space:
Riley was frustrated with his art project, tearing up his paper in distress. Instead of rushing to stop him or suggest alternatives, his dad simply sat beside him silently for a few moments, providing a calming presence. This pause allowed Riley to communicate his frustration about not getting the colors right.

Reflection as a Tool:

During a car ride, Oliver suddenly exclaimed, "Too much!" Instead of pressing him immediately for specifics, his mother took a deep breath and responded, "Something feels like it's too much for you. Let's figure it out together." This thoughtful pause and reflective statement gave Oliver a chance to point to the radio, signaling that the volume was too high for him.

Validating and Echoing to Show Understanding

Reassurance through Echo:

When Ellie mentioned, "The lights at school are too flashy," her dad mirrored her sentiment by saying, "You find the lights at school a bit too bright and flashy?" Ellie nodded, feeling understood, which opened a conversation about possible solutions.

Affirmation:

Liam often hesitated to join group activities. One day, he murmured, "It's too noisy with everyone." Instead of dismissing his concern or pushing him to participate, his teacher validated his feelings by echoing, "It sounds like you feel it's quite loud when everyone's together. We can find a quieter activity for you if you'd prefer."

These are just a few glimpses into the myriad situations where active listening can transform moments of distress into opportunities for connection and understanding. It's not just about solving problems but more about understanding the journey of the child, embracing their unique perspective, and validating their experiences.

***

Building Vocabulary for Emotions

Navigating the vast realm of human emotions can be a complex journey, even for those of us who've been on this Earth for decades. For our children, especially those on the autism spectrum, it can sometimes feel like deciphering a foreign language. As caregivers, it's our heartfelt duty to be their translators and teachers, helping them identify and articulate their feelings.

Starting with Basic Emotion Cards

Imagine you're learning a new language. Would you start with complex phrases or basic words? Similarly, when helping our children understand emotions, it's beneficial to begin with the basics. Start with emotion cards that depict clear, easily recognizable feelings such as happy, sad, angry, and scared. By using visual aids, children can make tangible connections between their internal feelings and external expressions.

Example: Little Emily, initially non-verbal, began using emotion cards to show her parents how she felt. When upset, she'd hand over the 'sad' card, and it became her bridge to express herself.

Gradually Introducing Complex Emotions

As children grow more comfortable with basic emotions, we can begin introducing them to nuanced feelings like frustration, excitement, disappointment, or curiosity. Just as a toddler moves from saying "big" to "enormous" or "tiny", our aim is to help them refine their emotional vocabulary.

Example: Nathan, after mastering the basic emotion cards, was introduced to feelings like 'jealousy' when he felt upset seeing his friend with a new toy. With time, he could express, "I feel jealous," making it easier for his parents to address the root cause.

Using Stories and Scenarios to Practice

Children resonate with stories. Through tales of characters experiencing various emotions, we can teach them how to relate those stories to their own lives. Narrate scenarios, use picture books, or even craft stories together, where characters navigate feelings, helping children identify and understand emotions in context.

Example: Every night, Olivia's dad would tell her a short story about animals in a forest. When the squirrel felt 'lonely' because it had no one to play with, or the bird felt 'proud' after building its first nest, Olivia began to associate those feelings with events in her own life.

By providing our children with the tools to understand and express their emotions, we are not just enhancing their communication but also enriching their emotional well-being.

It's akin to gifting them a compass for their journey through the intricate landscape of human feelings.

***

Collaborative Problem Solving:

There's a beautiful proverb that says, "If you want to go fast, go alone. If you want to go far, go together." In the journey of parenting, especially when navigating the intricate maze of autism, going together—hand in hand with our children—can make all the difference.

The Importance of Teamwork

Every parent has faced those moments—the ones where our child is deeply frustrated, where emotions boil over, and everything feels stuck. Instead of viewing these as obstacles, let's reimagine them as opportunities—chances for us to come alongside our child, kneel to their level, and say, "Let's figure this out together."

In doing so, we instill in them a deep-seated belief: that they're not alone in their struggles. That their voice matters in finding a solution. That together, we're a team.

Example: When Jake struggled with his homework, instead of just giving him the answers or letting him flounder, his mom would say, "Looks like this is tricky. How about we tackle it as a team?"

Breaking Down Problems into Manageable Steps

The world can sometimes feel overwhelming, like a giant jigsaw puzzle with too many pieces. Our role? To help our children see that even the most daunting problems can be broken down, piece by piece.

Start by identifying the core issue. Then, brainstorm possible solutions, and break them down into small, actionable steps. This process not only makes challenges feel more manageable but also imparts essential problem-solving skills.

Example: Sarah was overwhelmed with cleaning her room. Her dad broke it down: "Let's first pick up the toys, then the books, and finally, we'll make the bed together." Step by step, the task felt less intimidating.

Celebrating Solutions and Adaptability

Every solved problem, no matter how small, is a victory worth celebrating. By highlighting our children's achievements and adaptability, we reinforce their self-belief and resilience.

Example: After weeks of practice, Leo managed to tie his shoelaces independently. Instead of rushing out the door, his family took a moment to celebrate his accomplishment, emphasizing his perseverance and adaptability.

In every challenge lies the seed of growth. Collaborative problem-solving isn't just about fixing what's wrong; it's about nurturing resilience, fostering connection, and celebrating the beautiful dance of growing up. As we embark on this journey, let's remember that the strength of the team lies in each member and in the bond between them.

Chapter Five

Sensory Integration

Embracing Unique Sensory Experiences

"The sensory experiences of individuals with autism are more than mere symptoms; they are a way of life." - Dr. Stephen Shore

Every rustle of leaves, the hum of city traffic, the feel of a woolen sweater against the skin, the aroma of fresh-baked bread — these sensory experiences are integral threads in the rich tapestry of our daily lives. For many of us, they fade into the background, unnoticed. Yet, for children with autism, these sensations can take center stage, often playing out in vivid technicolor and high-definition sound.

Have you ever tried to focus on a task with loud music blaring in the background or attempted to sleep while an irritating tag on your pajama prickled your skin? These examples, in a minuscule way, give us a glimpse into the heightened sensory experiences some children with autism may encounter daily.

In this chapter, we will journey into the world of sensory integration. We'll delve deep, aiming to understand, empathize, and ultimately harness these unique sensory experiences to create a harmonious environment for our children.

Decoding Sensory Signals

Each child's sensory profile is as unique as a fingerprint. While one child may seek intense sensory experiences, another might shy away from them. By keenly observing, noting patterns, and understanding these signals, we can proactively tailor their environments and routines.

Example: Max loved the feeling of water but couldn't stand the sound of it gushing from the faucet. His parents began filling the tub before calling him for his bath, making the experience more enjoyable for him.

Creating Sensory Havens

Our homes, schools, and recreational spaces can transform into havens that respect and cater to our children's sensory needs. Simple adjustments like dimming lights, introducing weighted blankets, or creating quiet corners can make a world of difference.

Example: Zoe was hypersensitive to auditory stimuli. Her parents set up a 'quiet tent' in the living room filled with cushions, books, and soft toys. Whenever things got too loud, Zoe had a serene spot to retreat to.

Harnessing Sensory Strengths

Instead of merely navigating sensory challenges, we can also celebrate and harness sensory strengths. Many children with autism have incredibly refined sensory skills. This heightened perception can be channeled into creative and productive outlets.

Example: Arjun, with his keen sense of smell, developed a passion for cooking. He could distinguish ingredients by their aromas and loved experimenting with flavors.

Embracing sensory integration isn't just about managing sensory overload or challenges. It's a journey of discovery, of understanding each child's unique sensory map, and of creating experiences that not only accommodate but also celebrate these differences. By the end of this chapter, I hope to leave you with strategies, insights, and, most importantly, a deeper appreciation for the world of sensory experiences that our children live in every day.

***

Understanding Sensory Sensitivities

Imagine a world where the gentlest hum of a refrigerator becomes a roaring freight train or where the soft touch of a cotton shirt feels like sandpaper against the skin. For some children with autism, such sensory experiences are a daily reality. Their world, rich in sensory perceptions, offers a vivid and often overwhelming tapestry of sights, sounds, textures, and feelings. In our journey to gentle parenting, understanding these sensitivities is paramount.

The Science Behind Sensory Processing in Autism

The complexities of sensory processing in autism are akin to a captivating symphony where certain instruments play louder than others. Neurons and synapses in the autistic brain might process information differently than in neurotypical individuals. This can lead to heightened or diminished responses to sensory stimuli. While science continues to explore the intricacies of this area, what's clear is that our children's sensory experiences are profoundly unique.

For instance, while most of us can tune out the repetitive noise of a ticking clock, a child with autism might perceive it as an incessant drumbeat, impossible to ignore.

Recognizing Hypo and Hyper Sensitivities

Hypo-sensitivity (under-responsiveness) and hyper-sensitivity (over-responsiveness) are two sides of the sensory coin. A child who is hypo-sensitive might display an insatiable desire for certain stimuli, like spinning or seeking deep pressure. On the other hand, hyper-sensitive children might be overwhelmed by stimuli most would deem normal, such as the texture of certain foods or the feel of tags on clothing.

Consider this: Sam, a hypo-sensitive child, might revel in the feeling of mud between his toes, seeking that tactile sensation. In contrast, Ava, who is hyper-sensitive, might be brought to tears by the buzzing sound of overhead lights, feeling bombarded by the auditory input.

Tailoring Environments to Sensory Needs

With a deeper understanding of sensory sensitivities, we're better equipped to create environments that honor our children's unique needs. This might involve investing in sensory tools like weighted blankets, adjusting lighting in rooms, or creating quiet retreat spaces for moments of overwhelm.

For example, for Mia, who finds the bustling energy of family gatherings overwhelming due to her hyper-sensitivity, her parents crafted a cozy nook in her room with dimmed lights, soft cushions, and her favorite books. It became her sanctuary, a space to regroup and find calm.

In embracing our children's sensory journeys, we're not just making their worlds more comfortable; we're signaling to them that their experiences are valid, that they are understood, and most importantly, that they are unconditionally loved.

***

Sensory Play and Exploration

In our ever-evolving quest to better connect with our children, it's essential to remember that their worlds are often painted with broader sensory strokes than ours. The wind isn't just something that cools, the grass isn't simply green, and water isn't just wet. Each sensory encounter is a novel adventure, a chance to explore, and an opportunity to connect deeper. Sensory play, often seen as mere fun, is truly a window to understanding our children's unique sensory experiences and aiding their development.

Introducing Varied Textures, Sounds, and Experiences

Children with autism might sometimes be hesitant to explore different sensations due to sensory sensitivities. However, gentle introductions can be key. Start with what they love. If they adore the texture of rice grains, introduce them to similar but slightly different textures like lentils or beads. Play soft tunes if they're enamored by music and then gradually introduce various instruments' sounds. The beauty lies in observing their reactions and preferences and adapting accordingly.

Picture this: A sunny day outdoors, where Jamie feels the smoothness of pebbles, hears the rustling of leaves, and sees the shimmer of sunlight on water, exploring one sensation at a time, at his own pace.

Crafting Sensory Bins and Safe Spaces

One of the most delightful ways to indulge in sensory play is through sensory bins. These are containers filled with materials meant to stimulate one or more of the senses. Think of a large bin filled with sand, where hidden treasures await exploration. Or a container filled with water beads that provide a unique tactile sensation. The key is to ensure safety, ensuring the materials are non-toxic and appropriate for the child's age and development stage.

Imagine: Sarah's glee as she dives her hands into a sensory bin filled with cool, slippery spaghetti, dyed in vibrant, safe colors, each strand offering a new tactile experience.

Embracing the World Through Sensory Lenses

The beauty of sensory play is that it doesn't need to be confined to specific tools or settings. The world is a sensory playground! A simple walk in the park can become a myriad of experiences - the feeling of different terrains underfoot, the varied birdcalls, and the kaleidoscope of colors as seasons change.

Envision: Holding hands with Leo as you both close your eyes and feel the sun's warmth on your faces, breathing in the scent of blooming flowers, and simply being in that moment, feeling the world together.

In fostering sensory exploration, we're not just aiding our children's development; we're creating a bridge, a shared language of experience and emotion. As you embark on this sensory journey, cherish the laughter, the discoveries, and even the hesitations. For in these moments, connections are forged, and memories are etched in the heart's tapestry.

Let's delve deeper into sensory play and its facets, and I'll provide concrete examples to offer clarity:

Sensory Play and Exploration

1. Introducing Varied Textures, Sounds, and Experiences:

Every child with autism is unique in their sensory preferences. Tapping into this variety is a journey worth taking.

- **Textures:** Start with soft materials like cotton balls, gradually introducing other textures such as velvet, silk, and even burlap. Each texture can be explored through touch and play. For instance, create a "texture path" with different materials on the floor, guiding your child to walk or crawl over, and discuss how each feels underfoot.

- **Sounds:** Begin with familiar sounds, perhaps from their favorite songs or nature sounds. Slowly introduce new ones - the soft hum of a bee, the patter of rain, the rustle of paper. An activity could involve a "Sound Match" game, where you play various sounds, and your child matches them to the corresponding object or image.

- **Experiences:** Transform daily routines into sensory adventures. Bath time can be a sensory haven, with warm and cool water explorations, bubbles of different sizes, or even water-resistant toys of various textures and shapes.

2. Crafting Sensory Bins and Safe Spaces:

Sensory bins are all about controlled and concentrated sensory experiences.

- **Rice Sensory Bin:** Dye rice with food coloring and let your child explore the rainbow under their fingers. Add in scoopers, cups, and hidden toys for added fun and tactile discovery.

- **Nature Bin:** Fill a container with items from nature - pinecones, leaves, sticks, and stones. This bin becomes a microcosm of the outside world, allowing your child to explore without feeling overwhelmed.

- **Water Play:** Using a large plastic tub, introduce warm water and various items that float and sink. This not only stimulates touch but also introduces basic scientific concepts in a fun way.

3. Embracing the World Through Sensory Lenses:

The world around us provides innumerable opportunities for sensory exploration.

- **Nature Walks:** Walks can be transformed into sensory-rich experiences. Encourage your child to listen to the different sounds - from the crunch of dry leaves underfoot to the distant chirping of crickets. Let them touch tree barks, feeling the contrasts between rough and smooth, or play with the water at a nearby stream.

- **Grocery Store Visits:** Though some children may find grocery stores over-whelming, they can also be sensory treasure troves. Feel the coolness of the freezer section, the textures of fruits and vegetables, or even the scent from the bakery.

- **Home Explorations:** Even the familiar environment of the home is ripe for exploration. Create a 'Touch and Tell' game, where your child touches an object with their eyes closed and describes it, guessing what it might be.

In all these explorations, the key is to move at your child's pace, ensuring they feel safe and engaged. Celebrate every little sensory victory, and cherish the unique perspective your child brings into your world.

***

Managing Overstimulation

The world is a cascade of sights, sounds, smells, and sensations. For a child with autism, this cascade can sometimes feel more like a torrent, with waves that threaten to pull them under. Overstimulation isn't just about being "too sensitive" – it's a very real challenge that requires a compassionate, knowledgeable approach. Let's explore how you, as a parent or guardian, can be your child's anchor during these turbulent times.

Identifying Early Signs of Sensory Overwhelm:
Sensory overwhelm doesn't happen out of the blue. There are precursors, little signs that tell us the sea is getting choppy.

- **Change in Posture or Movement:** Your child might become unusually stiff or, conversely, may start to fidget excessively. Some children might cover their ears, shield their eyes, or even retreat to a corner.

- **Vocal Indications:** From sudden silence to increased volume or tone of voice, auditory changes can signal distress. They might start using repetitive phrases or sounds as a way to cope.

- **Emotional Shifts:** Look for signs of distress, such as increased anxiety, agitation, or even a sudden shift to being withdrawn.

Techniques for Grounding and Calming:

When the waves rise, your child needs an anchor, something to help them find their footing again.

- **Deep Pressure:** Weighted blankets, tight hugs, or even just being wrapped snugly in a regular blanket can provide immediate relief. The deep pressure is soothing and offers a sense of security.

- **Focused Breathing:** Guide your child to take deep, deliberate breaths. "Smell the flowers, blow out the candles" is a child-friendly way to teach this.

- **Designated Safe Spaces:** Having a go-to quiet spot, free from sensory triggers, can be invaluable. This space, stocked with favorite calming items, can act as a refuge during sensory storms.

Reflecting and Learning from Experiences:

Every challenge presents an opportunity to learn. And every episode of overstimulation holds insights into your child's sensory world.

- **Post-Event Discussions:** Once your child is calm, gently discuss what happened. Use simple language and encourage them to express how they feel.

- **Maintain a Journal:** Documenting triggers, environments, and successful calming techniques can be beneficial. Over time, patterns will emerge, and you can better predict and prevent potential overwhelm.

- **Involve the Child:** As they grow, children can become active participants in understanding their triggers. They can even be taught to recognize early signs themselves and take preemptive measures.

Creating Sensory Breaks and Retreats

In the orchestra of life, sometimes the instruments play too loudly, jumbling into a cacophony rather than a symphony. For children with autism, the world can often feel this way – an overwhelming barrage of sensory inputs. Sensory breaks, a brief respite from this sensory onslaught, can act as an interlude, bringing harmony back to their world. Let's delve deeper into these quiet sanctuaries.

The Philosophy Behind Sensory Breaks:

At the core of a sensory break is the idea of "recharging." Just as we take breaks during a strenuous physical task, sensory breaks offer a mental and emotional pause. This isn't about avoiding sensory experiences but allowing a child to process them at a pace that's comfortable for them.

Designing the Perfect Sensory Retreat:

Every child is unique, and their retreat should reflect their individual needs. Here are some ideas to get you started:

1. **The Cozy Corner:** Dedicate a small space, perhaps a corner of the child's room, filled with soft cushions, a bean bag, and comforting textures. Dimmed lights or a soft glow lamp can add to the serenity.

2. **Nature Nooks:** Nature has a calming effect. A small tent or canopy in the backyard, surrounded by the sounds of rustling leaves and chirping birds, can be a perfect getaway. For those without outdoor space, even a small indoor plant or a tabletop water fountain can introduce nature's tranquility.

3. **Music Refuge:** Create a playlist of soothing melodies. Headphones can help filter out external noise, letting the child immerse in the world of calming tunes. Alternatively, white noise machines or apps can also be effective.

4. **Artistic Outlets:** Some children find solace in expressing themselves. A corner with coloring books, clay, or even just paper and crayons can be therapeutic. Let it be a space of free expression, where the process is celebrated over the product.

5. **Textured Paradise:** Fill a bin with materials of varying textures – from soft sands to squishy gels, and even some cooling materials. This tactile experience can divert the child's attention, offering a sensory-rich yet controlled exploration.

Implementing Sensory Breaks in Daily Life:

It's essential to read the child's cues. When you notice signs of sensory overwhelm, gently guide them to their retreat. Over time, the child can even be taught to recognize when they need a break, fostering a sense of autonomy.

For those on the go, consider a portable sensory kit. A small pouch with a few calming items – perhaps a textured toy, a familiar scent, or even a favorite cloth – can be a lifesaver during outings.

Navigating the sensory intricacies of autism might seem daunting, but with patience, creativity, and love, it becomes a journey of discovery. Each sensory break and retreat is more than just an escape; it's a bridge toward understanding, connection, and growth.

In this journey, remember that you're not just managing sensory experiences; you're embracing a unique perspective of the world. With each challenge comes growth, understanding, and a bond that deepens between you and your child.

***

Encouraging Sensory Challenges

Walking through life, we often stumble upon paths less traveled, routes a tad bit thorny, or landscapes that are unfamiliar. These are our challenges, and like us, children with autism also face their unique sensory challenges. While their sensory experiences might sometimes seem overwhelming, with our guidance, these can turn into avenues for growth and discovery. Let's explore how to gently usher them into these sensory adventures.

The Delicate Balance of Challenge and Comfort:

Before diving in, it's essential to understand that challenges should be just that – challenging but not overwhelming. The goal is not to thrust them into a sensory tornado but to introduce them to gentle breezes, which might seem stormy to them but are manageable with support.

Starting Small with Gradual Exposure:
Imagine dipping your toes into a cold pool. At first, it sends shivers, but with time, you acclimate. Similarly, begin with short, controlled exposures to challenging sensations. Maybe it's the roughness of a woolen sweater or the hum of a crowded place. Brief encounters, followed by comfort and reassurance, can slowly build tolerance.

Celebrate Every Brave Step:
It's not about how big or small the challenge is; it's about the courage to face it. Every time your child confronts a sensory challenge, celebrate it. Applause, words of affirmation, or even a small reward can go a long way in reinforcing their bravery.

Adapting Challenges as They Grow:
As they mature, their sensory landscape will evolve. What was once a sensory mountain might now be a mere molehill, and new mountains might appear. Keep observing, understanding, and adjusting the challenges accordingly. This dynamic approach ensures that they are always growing, but at a pace that respects their unique journey.

Seeking Feedback and Reflecting:
Post every sensory challenge, and have a little chat. What did they feel? Was it too much, or do they think they can handle a bit more next time? This not only gives you valuable feedback but also involves them in the decision-making process, making them active participants in their growth journey.

Lastly, remember that every child's sensory map is different. Comparisons are not just unnecessary; they can be detrimental. Instead, focus on their individual progress, their milestones, and the joyous moments when they surprise themselves with their own resilience.

With patience, love, and a dash of creativity, these sensory challenges can become the stepping stones to a world of sensory wonders, waiting to be embraced and celebrated.

***

Integrating Sensory Tools

As we journey through the expansive world of sensory experiences with our children, sometimes we come across bumpy roads or sudden storms. That's where our sensory tools come into play - they're like the trusty umbrella in a downpour or the cushioned shoes on a rocky path. These tools, ranging from weighted blankets to playful fidgets, can be life-changers in navigating the sensory maze. Here's a closer look at how these tools can be integrated into our daily lives, making every sensory experience a tad bit smoother.

The Comforting Embrace of Weighted Blankets:
Have you ever felt the soothing hug of a thick quilt on a cold day? A weighted blanket offers a similar experience but magnified. For children with autism, it can be like a gentle, reassuring hug during times of distress. The deep pressure it provides has a calming effect, reducing anxiety and aiding sleep. If your child has never tried one, start with a lighter weight and see how they respond.

Choosing the Right Weight:
Start by selecting a blanket that's approximately 10% of your child's body weight. This ensures comfort while providing the needed deep pressure sensation. Experiment and adjust as needed.

Finding the Right Material:
Blankets come in various fabrics - from cooling cotton for those who run hot, to plush minky dots for those who crave tactile stimulation. Let your child touch and choose.

Fidget Away the Stress:
Children with autism often find solace in repetitive motions or sensations. Fidget tools, with their diverse textures, movements, and mechanisms, can be a fantastic outlet. They not only help in focusing but also offer a sensory escape when things get overwhelming. Keep a variety on hand - from spinners to textured bands - and let your child find their favorite.

DIY Fidgets:

From beads and strings to create simple necklaces, to balloons filled with flour or rice for a squeezable hand toy, there's no limit to what you can craft at home.

Fidget Jewelry:
Available in stores and online, fidget jewelry like rings, necklaces, or bracelets can be both stylish and functional. They can be discreetly used in public settings like schools without drawing attention.

Crafting a Sensory Toolkit for On-the-Go:
While at home, we can control the sensory environment to a large extent. But what about those unpredictable outdoor scenarios? That's where a sensory toolkit comes in handy. A small bag with a few essential items - perhaps a fidget tool, some noise-canceling earphones, or a familiar soft fabric - can be a lifesaver during unplanned sensory challenges.

Pocket-Size Calm:
Consider small items that fit into pockets: smooth stones for grounding, mini aroma therapy diffusers with calming scents, or textured cards that can be discreetly rubbed.

Digital Aids:
Load a tablet or smartphone with calming apps, like bubble pop games or white noise generators. Ensure you have soft, noise-canceling headphones if your child is sensitive to sound.

Keep It Fun, Keep It Accessible:
Remember, these tools should never feel like a chore or a medical intervention. The more fun and engaging they are, the more likely your child will naturally gravitate towards them. Customize them, get them in your child's favorite colors, or make them together as a DIY project. Keep them easily accessible, maybe in a dedicated corner or a special box, so they can be reached whenever the need arises.

Invite Siblings or Friends:
Sometimes, having a sibling or friend use a sensory tool can make it more enticing. This not only promotes the tool but fosters a shared experience.

In the grand tapestry of sensory experiences, these tools are the threads that can help in weaving a smoother, more harmonious pattern. They're not just aids but companions, each with its unique role in making the sensory journey more enjoyable and manageable.

So, as you integrate them into your daily routine, do it with an open heart, lots of creativity, and a sprinkle of fun.

Here are ten items to consider including in your on-the-go sensory toolkit:

1. **Weighted Lap Pad:** A smaller version of a weighted blanket, it provides deep pressure and can be easily folded into a bag. It's useful during car rides or while seated in public places.

2. **Fidget Toys:** From simple silicone poppers to more complex puzzle-like toys, these can help manage anxiety and keep hands occupied.

3. **Noise-Canceling Headphones:** Perfect for situations where the environment might get too noisy, such as crowded areas or events with sudden loud sounds.

4. **Textured Tactile Toys:** Items like soft brushes, textured rubber mats, or even plush toys can provide a soothing tactile experience.

5. **Chewelry:** Jewelry made from safe, chewable material. It serves both a functional purpose for those who need oral stimulation and a fashionable one.

6. **Aromatherapy Roller or Inhaler:** Scents like lavender or chamomile can be calming. Having a roller or inhaler allows discreet application in high-stress situations.

7. **Visual Stim Tools:** Liquid motion timers, glitter jars, or kaleidoscopes can be calming and captivating, providing a focus point when overwhelmed.

8. **Compact Umbrella or Hat:** For kids who might find direct sunlight or overhead lights too intense, having something to create a small shade can be beneficial.

9. **Small, Soft Blanket or Cloth:** Something familiar and comforting from home that can be draped or held for solace.

10. **Pocket-Sized Photo Album:** Filled with pictures of loved ones, familiar places, or even cue cards that can help communicate feelings or needs when words might be challenging.

Always keep this toolkit in a handy spot, like the car or a go-to bag, so it's within reach when you need it. Regularly check and rotate items based on your child's evolving preferences and needs.

Chapter Six

Social Navigation

Fostering Connections and Friendships

"To understand the world of someone with autism, you must first understand their world of feelings and senses." - Paul Isaacs

In the words of Temple Grandin, "I am different, not less." Autism might make social interactions challenging, but it certainly doesn't diminish the desire or the capacity for meaningful connections. This chapter delves into the beautiful journey of helping our children bridge their unique world with the wider social universe.

• **Recognizing the Spectrum of Social Comfort:**
Every child with autism has a different threshold and comfort level when it comes to social situations. From the child who enjoys being around peers but struggles with initiating conversation, to the one who feels overwhelmed in large gatherings, understanding this spectrum is the first step. Here, we'll discuss how to recognize these cues and the ways in which they can change over time.

• **Crafting a Safe Social Framework:**
It's essential to create environments where children feel safe to express themselves, make mistakes, and learn. This might mean setting up playdates with understanding friends, joining supportive social groups, or attending special workshops. In this section, we explore avenues to create these nurturing social frameworks.

• **Tailoring Social Skill Lessons:**
Not all social skills are intuitive for children on the spectrum. Sometimes, they need

explicit instruction on various nuances. From understanding non-verbal cues, to taking turns in a conversation, to expressing themselves effectively, we'll explore strategies to teach these skills in a way that feels natural and engaging.

• Using Stories and Role-Playing:

Stories and role-playing exercises can be instrumental in teaching children about social situations. They offer a safe platform to understand scenarios, empathize with characters, and practice responses. Here, we'll share some exemplary stories and role-playing techniques that have proven to be effective.

• Celebrating Uniqueness in Social Interactions:

While adapting to societal norms is valuable, it's equally important to celebrate and embrace the unique ways in which our children communicate and interact. In this concluding section of the chapter, we'll discuss the importance of teaching our children the value of their uniqueness and how it contributes positively to the world around them.

Through this chapter, our aim is to equip you, dear reader, with a blend of strategies and heartwarming stories, enabling your child to form genuine connections and friendships, all while honoring their unique essence.

***

Building Social Stories

"Every person has a story, and every interaction is a chapter of that story."

Navigating the intricate web of social interactions can often feel like deciphering an intricate novel for children with autism. But what if we could simplify these interactions into relatable, digestible stories? That's the magic of social stories. Let's journey together into this world of narrative teaching.

Introducing Scenarios through Narrative:

Think of a situation that might be perplexing for your child—perhaps sharing toys, or understanding why someone is crying. By crafting a simple story, using relatable characters or even real-life individuals they know, we can give context to these situations. For instance, "Tommy Turtle loves his green toy car. But one day, his friend Fiona Frog wanted to play with it. Tommy remembered how happy he felt when he shared his sandwich last week and decided to let Fiona have a turn." Through such narratives, abstract concepts become tangible tales.

1. **Visit to the Doctor:** Craft a story about "Danny Dragon's Friendly Doctor Visit." Describe the waiting room, the kind nurse, and the doctor's gentle methods. This can prepare your child for what to expect and alleviate anxiety.

2. **First Day of School:** Use a tale like "Penny Penguin's New School Adventure." Highlight the fun parts of school, from making new friends to engaging in fun activities, thus transforming apprehension into excitement.

Role-playing and Practicing Responses:

Once we've introduced a scenario, it's time to bring it to life. Together, you and your child can enact the story. Maybe you can be Tommy, and your child can be Fiona. Role-playing is a safe space for them to understand, experiment, and even make mistakes. It's a rehearsal for real life, making unknown situations familiar and less intimidating.

1. **Birthday Party Attendance:** You can set up a mini birthday scene at home with stuffed toys as guests. Practice singing "Happy Birthday" and sharing cake. By role-playing, you help familiarize your child with the sequence of events and expected behaviors.

2. **Responding to Greetings:** Together, act out scenarios where someone says "hello" or waves. Let your child practice responses, whether it's waving back, smiling, or saying "hi."

Adapting Stories for Varied Social Settings:

The beauty of social stories is in their adaptability. Whether it's prepping for a visit to the dentist, a day at school, or a playdate at the park, we can craft stories tailored to fit any setting. For instance, if a visit to a crowded supermarket is on the cards, we can create a story about "Lenny Lion's Adventure in the Jungle Market," making a potentially overwhelming outing an exciting quest.

1. **Supermarket Adventures:** Instead of the simple 'Lenny Lion' story, we can add details. "Lenny Lion made a list of fruits he wanted: bananas, apples, and oranges. In the Jungle Market, he found them all, and even helped an old owl reach a high shelf." This not only sets expectations but also instills good behaviors.

2. **Playground Etiquette:** Craft a story titled "Holly Hedgehog's Day at the Playground." Detail how Holly waited her turn for the slide, asked politely to join a game and made a new friend. By adapting the story to this setting, you're preparing your child for proper playground decorum.

Building social stories is not just about teaching; it's about connecting. It's about taking a walk in our children's shoes and hand-in-hand, showing them the way. It's about understanding, and adapting, and most importantly, it's about making every child feel seen, heard, and valued in their unique way.

***

Encouraging Group Activities

Navigating group activities can sometimes seem like venturing into uncharted waters for a child with autism. Yet, when approached thoughtfully, these shared experiences can be a treasure trove of learning, joy, and connection. Let's embark on this journey together.

Selecting Suitable Group Dynamics:
When choosing a group activity, it's essential to consider the setting and the children involved. Not all group activities are created equal. For instance, some kids may thrive in smaller groups where individual interactions are more manageable and less overwhelming. Activities like crafting circles, book clubs, or small playdates could be ideal. On the other hand, some children may prefer groups where they can blend in a bit more, like in larger art classes or music groups where the focus is shared amongst many.

- **Book Clubs:** Jennifer's son, Ethan, always had a fascination with trains. So,

Jennifer set up a small book club with a few other children, centered around train-themed stories. Not only did it cater to Ethan's love for trains, but it also provided a calm setting to enhance his social interactions.

- **Crafting Circles:** When Ella noticed her daughter, Lily, meticulously stringing beads together, she organized a weekend crafting circle. Here, children would come together and create bead necklaces, bracelets, or simple patterns. The repetitive nature of the task was soothing, and it gave the kids something to focus on as they chatted.

Building on Shared Interests and Passions:

Harness the power of shared passions. When children unite over a common interest, bonds form more naturally. Perhaps it's a Lego building group, where each child contributes to creating a fantastic city. Or maybe it's an animal lovers' club where kids share stories of their pets and learn about different animals. By aligning group activities with their existing passions, you set the stage for genuine enthusiasm and engagement.

- **Lego Building Group:** Leo, who is a Lego enthusiast, was elated when his parents found a local Lego enthusiasts club. They'd have challenges like "build a bridge" or "construct an animal," allowing Leo to interact with peers who shared his fervor for Lego.

- **Animal Lovers' Club:** Mia, who was always fascinated by the birds outside her window, was introduced to a local bird-watching group. Together, the children would learn about different birds, listen to their calls, and occasionally, take trips to bird sanctuaries.

Emphasizing the Joy of Participation Over Competition:

In our competitive world, it's easy to lose sight of the intrinsic joy of simply participating. But for our children, especially those with autism, the emphasis should always be on the enjoyment of the activity rather than winning or being the best. Suppose it's a community sports day. Instead of focusing on who runs the fastest, we could celebrate everyone's participation with a colorful ribbon or a cheerful chant. In a group painting session, instead of judging the best artwork, highlight the unique beauty of every child's creation.

- **Community Sports Day:** During the local community's sports day, there was a shift from traditional races. Instead, they had events like "Silly Walks Parade" where children were encouraged to walk in the funniest ways they could think of. Everyone cheered, and every child received a ribbon for their unique walk.

- **Group Painting Session:** At Ben's school, they had a monthly painting session. There was no theme; kids were simply given paints and let loose on large canvases. At the end of the session, instead of individual praises, the teacher would highlight how all the paintings together made the room brighter and more vibrant.

Remember, the goal isn't to mold our children into social butterflies overnight. It's about providing them with opportunities to connect, share, and grow. It's about teaching them that, in the vast tapestry of human interactions, they have their own unique thread to contribute. And when woven together with care, understanding, and patience, the result is a beautiful mosaic of connections and friendships.

***

Cultivating Empathy and Understanding

Empathy, often described as the ability to walk in another's shoes, is a cornerstone of human connection. For children on the autism spectrum, understanding emotions and connecting with others might sometimes be a challenge, but it's certainly not out of reach. Let's delve into how you can help your child develop these crucial skills:

Teaching Perspective-Taking:
Imagine this: It's a sunny afternoon, and you're sitting with your child, Sarah. Together, you watch as a child at the park drops their ice cream. You gently ask Sarah, "How do you think the child feels right now?" Sarah might initially respond with, "Sad because the ice cream is gone." This is a start! Over time, with more of these observations, you can guide Sarah to a deeper understanding, like recognizing disappointment, regret, or embarrassment. These daily, real-life examples become lessons in perspective-taking.

Using Multimedia to Explain Emotions and Reactions:
Children often resonate with stories, songs, and visual tales. Think of a time when Jack watched an animated movie. Remember when the main character felt left out? You could pause the movie and discuss with Jack what's happening. "See how he's sitting alone while everyone is playing? How do you think he feels?" Movies, books, and even songs offer rich tapestries of emotions. Over time, Jack begins to recognize and name these emotions, gradually understanding their nuances.

Celebrating Acts of Kindness and Connection:
Every act of kindness, no matter how small, is worth celebrating. When Lucy shares her toys with her sibling, make a note to praise her. "Lucy, it was so kind of you to share your teddy. It made your brother smile." Over time, Lucy begins to equate sharing with happiness, cultivating a natural inclination toward empathy.

Keep in mind, that the journey to cultivate empathy and understanding is continuous. Each day offers countless teachable moments. What's imperative is our presence, patience, and belief in our child's incredible capacity for growth and connection. Remember, the roots of empathy are often found in the simplest acts, and with consistent guidance, they grow deep and strong, helping your child navigate the rich tapestry of human emotions and relationships.

***

Navigating Peer Relationships

Ah, the intricate dance of friendships and peer relationships. From the early years when "friendship" might simply mean someone to play with at the playground, to the more complex relationships of adolescence and beyond, friendships provide a rich ground for emotional and social growth. For children with autism, while the dance steps might be different, the music is the same – it's all about connection, understanding, and mutual respect.

Introducing the Concept of Friendship:

Imagine sitting with your child, Ben, flipping through a family photo album. You come across a picture of you and your best friend from childhood. "See him, Ben? That's my friend, Alex. We did everything together – just like you and Jamie." Through personal stories and daily observations, you slowly build an understanding of what friendship looks like. Over time, Ben starts recognizing and seeking those connections, whether it's a shared love for drawing or just the simple joy of laughter.

Role-playing Common Social Interactions:

The playground. The classroom. Birthday parties. These are the arenas where social interactions play out. But instead of just diving in, how about a rehearsal? Think of it as a playful act. Maybe today, you and Mia are at a birthday party. You're another child, and you've just received a gift. How should Mia react? How would she feel if she was the one receiving the gift? Role-playing not only prepares Mia for real-life scenarios but also provides a safe space to navigate the ebb and flow of social dynamics.

Celebrating the Joys and Lessons of Relationships:

Friendships aren't just about the sunny days; they come with their share of rainy days too. And that's okay. When Ellie has a tiff with her friend because both want the same toy, it's an opportunity. Later, when the emotions have settled, a gentle conversation can ensue. "Remember when you both wanted the toy? It's tough, isn't it? But it's also how we learn." The next time, Ellie might just surprise you with her solution.

In the end, it's essential to remember that while the paths might differ, the destination remains the same. Peer relationships, with all their challenges and joys, serve as invaluable life lessons. They teach us about ourselves, about others, and about the intricate dance of human connection. And every dance, no matter the steps, is beautiful in its own right.

***

Preparing for Social Challenges

Every journey has its bumps in the road. Just as we pack a first aid kit for physical wounds, we need to equip our children with tools for the emotional and social scrapes they might encounter. Navigating the social realm, particularly for a child with autism, is like venturing into an ever-changing maze. The walls shift, the paths twist, and sometimes, there are dead ends. But with preparation, understanding, and reflection, we can make this journey smoother and more rewarding.

Equipping with Tools for Conflict Resolution:
It's a sunny day and your child, Aiden, is building sandcastles in the park. Suddenly, another child comes over and knocks it down. Tears well up in Aiden's eyes. Here lies an opportunity for teaching. We can give Aiden tools, like words to express himself: "I feel sad when my castle is destroyed. Can we build one together?" or methods to walk away and seek comfort. Remember that toy or a comfort object he never leaves home without? It's not just a toy; it's a tool. In moments of conflict, it can be the anchor he holds onto, allowing him to process his emotions and return to a state of calm.

1. **Emotion Cards:** These are cards with faces depicting various emotions. When a situation becomes too overwhelming for verbal expression, children can use these cards to communicate their feelings.

2. **Breathing Techniques:** Teach simple techniques like "Take 5" where the child takes five deep breaths in and out, visualizing inflating a balloon and then letting the air out slowly.

3. **'I Feel' Statements:** Encourage children to use statements like, "I feel hurt when you don't share with me," to express emotions without casting blame.

Role-playing Challenging Social Scenarios:
Let's step into the world of make-believe. Today, you and Clara are classmates. She's sharing a story, but you interrupt her. How does she react? Role-playing doesn't just prepare Clara for real-life situations; it also empowers her. Over time, as you play out more scenarios, she gains confidence, knowing she's equipped with strategies to handle them. From managing interruptions to experiencing the complexities of group dynamics, this safe space of role-play helps her explore and understand.

1. **Playground Dynamics:** Mimic a scenario at the playground, where one child hogs the swing, leading to a confrontation. Discuss potential solutions, such as asking politely for a turn or seeking another activity and returning later.

2. **Classroom Situations:** Act out scenarios like being called upon in class and not knowing the answer. Discuss feelings of embarrassment and strategies to cope, like saying, "I need more time to think," or asking a friend for help.

3. **Online Interactions:** In today's digital age, role-playing online interactions is crucial. Discuss appropriate online behavior, and how to handle cyberbullying or uncomfortable situations.

Reflecting and Learning from Experiences:

After a playdate, as you and Noah are driving back home, it's the perfect time for a chat. "Remember when Jake took away your toy? How did that make you feel?" This isn't about pointing out mistakes. It's about reflection. It's an opportunity to understand Noah's perspective, validate his feelings, and maybe suggest alternative approaches. It's a gentle reminder that every experience, whether joyful or challenging, offers its lesson.

1. **Daily Debrief:** Establish a routine where, at the end of the day, you discuss one positive social interaction and one challenging one. Over tea or a light snack, celebrate the wins and address the challenges.

2. **Emotion Diary:** Provide your child with a journal where they can draw or write about their feelings, making it easier to pinpoint triggers and celebrate positive social achievements.

3. **Social Interaction Role Reversal:** Let your child narrate a social situation to you, then reverse roles. You act as the child, and they take on the role of a peer or adult. This not only promotes empathy but helps the child see situations from different viewpoints.

The world of social interactions is vast and unpredictable, but with love, patience, and the right tools, our children can not only navigate it but also thrive within it. As they grow, they won't just be learning how to handle social challenges; they'll be teaching us about resilience, perseverance, and the boundless capacity of the human spirit to connect and understand.

Chapter Seven

Learning and Growth

Educational Success with Gentle Parenting

"Every student can learn, just not on the same day, or the same way." - George Evans

Education is more than just acquiring knowledge; it's a journey of self-discovery, understanding the world around us, and finding one's place within it. For children with autism, the academic arena can often be challenging, overwhelming, or even frustrating. But with the principles of gentle parenting, we can bridge the gap between learning challenges and success. This chapter will explore the beautiful symbiosis of educational growth and gentle parenting, ensuring that your child not only learns but also thrives.

Recognizing Individual Learning Styles:

Every child, autistic or not, has a unique way they grasp and process information. Some are visual learners, others auditory, and still, some prefer hands-on experiences. Recognize these styles and mold the learning process around them. For instance:

- **Visual Learners:** Use charts, diagrams, and visual aids.

- **Auditory Learners:** Introduce rhymes, songs, and verbal instructions.

- **Kinesthetic Learners:** Implement hands-on activities, experiments, and physical movement.

Creating a Positive Learning Environment at Home:

A safe and comfortable learning environment can significantly impact how effectively a child with autism can study. Here's how to do it:

- Ensure the study space is free from distractions, but also sensory-friendly. Soft lighting, calming colors, and noise-cancelling headphones can be beneficial.

- Have a structured routine but be flexible enough to allow breaks when needed.

- Use tools like visual schedules, timers, and reward charts to structure study sessions.

Collaborating with Educators:

Open communication with your child's teachers and therapists is crucial. By understanding the classroom dynamics and the teaching methodologies employed, you can better support your child's learning journey at home. Moreover, educators can also benefit from understanding your child's specific needs and triggers.

Using Technology as an Ally:

There are numerous apps and software tailored to aid children with autism in their learning journey. From interactive stories that improve comprehension to fun math games that solidify basic concepts, technology can be a significant ally.

Celebrating Achievements, Big and Small:

Every milestone, no matter how tiny, is a testament to your child's perseverance and your dedication. It could be mastering a new word, completing a puzzle, or even participating in a group activity in school. Celebrate them with words of encouragement, small rewards, or even just quality time spent together.

Conclusion:

The journey of education, especially for children with autism, is paved with challenges. But with patience, understanding, and the principles of gentle parenting, it can also be one filled with joy, discovery, and immense growth. Always remember that the goal is not just academic success but fostering a lifelong love for learning.

***

Crafting an Individualized Learning Plan

Every child is unique, and so is their learning journey. The age-old "one-size-fits-all" approach to education often leaves many children, especially those with unique needs like autism, feeling misunderstood or left behind. An Individualized Learning Plan (ILP) acts as a roadmap, tailored specifically for your child, ensuring they get the most out of their educational experiences. Let's delve into how you can create a meaningful ILP for your child.

Recognizing Strengths and Interests:

Before we even begin to create an educational plan, it's vital to understand the child at the core. What excites them? What are they naturally good at? Perhaps your child has an affinity for numbers and patterns, or maybe they are drawn to the arts, expressing themselves through music, painting, or dance.

Start by observing your child during their free play or during routine tasks. Take note of the activities they naturally gravitate towards. These are clues to their innate strengths and passions. Celebrate these strengths and incorporate them into the learning process. If your child loves music, perhaps math lessons can be taught through rhythm and song. If they adore nature, science and biology can be explored in the great outdoors.

Setting Achievable Goals:

With the strengths and interests identified, it's time to set some goals. However, these shouldn't be broad, overarching goals. Instead, focus on specific, achievable milestones. If your child struggles with reading, for instance, don't merely set a goal like "Improve reading." Instead, aim for something tangible like, "Read a five-page story aloud without assistance."

Remember, these goals should challenge your child but not overwhelm them. The aim is to build confidence and celebrate progress, however incremental.

Collaborating with Educators and Therapists:

You're not alone in this journey. Teachers, special educators, therapists, and counselors can offer invaluable insights into crafting an effective ILP. They can provide feedback on the goals set, suggest suitable resources, and even recommend strategies that have proven successful in the past.

Arrange regular meetings with these professionals. Share your insights, listen to theirs, and together, create an evolving plan that adapts as your child grows and learns.

Conclusion:

Crafting an ILP is more than just setting academic goals. It's about understanding and celebrating your child's uniqueness, ensuring their educational journey is as enriching and enjoyable as possible. With patience, collaboration, and a deep understanding of your child, you can pave the way for a fulfilling and empowering learning experience.

***

Fostering a Love for Learning

Every child is born with an innate curiosity, a wonder for the world around them. Think back to those early days when your child's eyes would light up at the sight of a floating soap bubble or their persistent attempts to stack blocks, undeterred by countless tumbles. This raw enthusiasm, this genuine love for learning, is one of the most beautiful gifts a child possesses. As caregivers and parents, it's our privilege and responsibility to nurture this gift, especially in children with unique needs like autism, who might interact with the world a little differently. Here's how we can cultivate and keep that spark alive.

Introducing Topics Through Passion and Interest:

The quickest way to a child's heart and mind is through their passions. If your child has an affinity for animals, use that as a gateway into various subjects. Lions can introduce the continents they roam, the numbers that represent their pride, or the storybooks that narrate their adventures. By aligning learning topics with their passions, you're not just teaching a subject; you're providing an experience, one that they will eagerly dive into.

- **Nature Obsessions:** Many children find solace in the rhythms of nature. If your child is drawn to the outdoors, organize nature walks, create a bird-watching journal, or start a modest backyard garden. For a child passionate about stars, a simple telescope can introduce them to the wonders of the universe.

- **Tech Whizzes:** For those engrossed in technology, leverage their interest by introducing them to educational apps or coding games. Their love for screens can be channeled positively into creating their own small animations or understanding the science behind their favorite video game.

- **Bookworm Ventures:** If your child loses themselves in stories, dive deeper. Explore the history behind a certain tale or the geography of where it's set. A story about pirates can segue into maritime history or oceanography.

Emphasizing the Journey Over Outcomes:

In today's outcome-driven society, it's easy to get fixated on results. But for our children, especially those on the autism spectrum, the learning process is far more crucial than the end result. Maybe it took them longer to grasp a math concept, but in that journey, they learned perseverance. Perhaps their science project didn't win at the school fair, but they discovered the joy of experimentation. Celebrate these moments, these lessons. Let them know it's okay to make mistakes, to be imperfect. It's the journey, the effort, and the will to try that truly counts.

- **Artistic Pursuits:** Let's say your child takes an interest in painting but gets frustrated when their work doesn't mirror their vision. Rather than focusing on the finished piece, immerse them in the process. Discuss the feel of the brush, the blend of colors, and the joy of creation.

- **Sports Endeavors:** Maybe your child joins a community soccer team but struggles with coordination. Instead of fixating on scoring goals, celebrate their teamwork, their improving stamina, or their understanding of the game's rules.

Celebrating Curiosity and Exploration:

Children ask questions. A lot of them. And sometimes, these questions can catch us off guard. "Why is the sky blue?" "How does the rain come down?" Instead of offering a quick reply or, at times, dismissing them as trivial, dive deep. Explore these questions together. Visit the library, conduct mini-experiments at home, or watch educational videos. Turn their queries into mini-adventures, quests for knowledge. By doing so, you're reinforcing the idea that their questions, their curiosity, are valuable and worth exploring.

- **Kitchen Experiments:** The next time they ask, "Why does water boil?", rather than a quick reply, make it a kitchen science day. Explore different states of matter, learn about temperatures, or even make homemade ice cream to explain freezing points.

- **"What If" Journals:** Maintain a journal where you jot down every "What if" question they ask. Dedicate a day of the week to explore one of those questions in depth, whether it's through research, experiments, or field trips.

- **DIY Kits:** Transform their questions into hands-on learning. If they're curious about how plants grow, create a DIY planting kit. For queries about electricity, a basic circuit kit can be enlightening.

Conclusion:

Fostering a love for learning isn't about academic achievements or ticking boxes in a curriculum. It's about embracing and fueling the innate curiosity within every child. It's about creating an environment where questions are welcomed, effort is celebrated, and learning becomes a joyful, lifelong adventure. As you journey with your child, remember: it's not about filling a vessel but igniting a flame.

***

Incorporating Multi-Sensory Learning

Learning isn't a one-size-fits-all endeavor. Each child is a universe of interests, strengths, and unique ways they engage with the world. And especially for children on the autism spectrum, conventional classroom methods may not always resonate. So, how do we ensure they not only learn but relish the process? The key lies in multi-sensory learning. Let's delve deeper into this concept.

1. Tapping into Varied Learning Styles:

We often hear of children being auditory, visual, or kinesthetic learners. But the truth is, most children are a mix of all these and more.

- **Auditory Adventures:** Introduce topics through storytelling, rhymes, or even songs. Audiobooks can also be a wonderful resource, allowing your child to absorb information through listening.

- **Visual Voyages:** Flashcards, diagrams, mind maps, and color-coded notes can be immensely beneficial for visual learners. Educational videos or apps that explain concepts through animation can also be a hit.

- **Kinesthetic Quests:** For those who learn best by 'doing', transform lessons into physical activities. For instance, if you're teaching math, use body movements to explain concepts like addition or subtraction.

2. Using Tools, Manipulatives, and Hands-On Experiences:

Hands-on learning can transform abstract concepts into tangible experiences.

- **Math Manipulatives:** Use counters, beads, or even building blocks to elucidate mathematical concepts.

- **Science Experiments:** Kits are available that allow children to build circuits, create chemical reactions, or even observe live creatures like ants or caterpillars up close.

- **Literary Adventures:** Instead of just reading a story, how about acting it out? Create a little stage at home, use props, and let your child immerse themselves in the narrative.

3. Ensuring Comprehension and Retention:

Merely presenting information isn't enough; we must ensure it's understood and remembered.

- **Recap Rituals:** At the end of a learning session, engage in a quick recap. This could be a discussion, a mini-quiz, or even a creative expression of what's been learned.

- **Teach Back:** One of the best ways to gauge understanding is to have your child teach the concept back to you. It allows them to process the information and articulate it in their own words.

- **Consistent Reinforcement:** Periodically revisit topics. Use varied mediums each time to ensure concepts are firmly cemented in their minds.

By embracing multi-sensory learning, we're not just accommodating different learning styles; we're celebrating them. We're saying, "I see you, I understand you, and I'm here to make learning an exhilarating journey for you." And in that process, we're not just imparting knowledge, but fostering a deep-seated love for discovery.

***

Managing Educational Challenges

Every journey has its bumps and detours. The realm of education, as enriching as it is, also comes with its own set of challenges, especially for children on the autism spectrum. But the beauty lies not in eliminating these challenges, but in managing them, turning them into stepping stones rather than stumbling blocks. So, let's navigate this intricate path together.

Recognizing Potential Stressors and Triggers:

Awareness is the first step. Before we can address challenges, we need to recognize them.

- **Transitions and Changes:** A sudden switch in activities, unexpected changes in the school routine, or even a substitute teacher can be unsettling for some children.

- **Sensory Overloads:** The school bell, the bustling cafeteria, or even the fluorescent lights can be overstimulating.

- **Social Struggles:** Group activities, unstructured playtimes, or simply understanding social cues can become sources of stress.

It's crucial to maintain an open line of communication with educators, therapists, and most importantly, with your child. Regular check-ins can help pinpoint triggers before they escalate.

Creating a Supportive and Adaptable Learning Environment:

Once we're aware of the challenges, the next step is to craft an environment where learning can thrive.

- **Personalized Learning Spaces:** If sensory overload is a concern, perhaps a quiet corner with dimmed lights, noise-cancelling headphones, or even a soft rug can make a difference.

- **Flexible Scheduling:** If transitions are tough, visual schedules or timers can help. Introducing changes with a heads-up and a quick preparatory discussion can also ease the process.

- **Collaborative Efforts:** Work closely with educators. Perhaps your child needs short breaks between tasks or prefers verbal instructions over written ones. The goal is to tailor the learning experience to your child's unique needs.

Celebrating Progress and Effort:

In the grand tapestry of education, it's not just the milestones but every tiny stitch of effort that counts.

- **Effort Over Outcomes:** A math problem might take longer for one child than another, but the perseverance shown deserves applause. Celebrate the process, the grit, the tenacity.

- **Visual Progress Trackers:** Be it a sticker chart, a progress journal, or even a digital app, having a tangible representation of progress can be immensely motivating.

- **Reflection Time:** Spend time together reflecting on the week. Discuss the highs, the lows, and everything in between. And always, always end on a positive note.

In essence, managing educational challenges is about weaving a safety net of understanding, adaptability, and unwavering support. It's about reminding our children, time and again, that while the path might be tough, they're tougher, and they're never walking alone. We're right there, cheering them on, every step of the way.

***

Transitioning Between Educational Phases

Change is an inevitable part of life, and in the educational journey, it's often marked by transitions—moving from preschool to kindergarten, elementary to middle school, and so on. Each transition comes with its own set of joys, challenges, and lessons. For children with autism, these transitions might be a tad more intricate, demanding a little extra care and preparation. Here's how we can smooth out these shifts.

Preparing for School Transitions:

The first step in any transition is anticipation. Preparation can drastically reduce anxiety.

- **Open Discussions:** Begin by talking about the upcoming transition months in advance. Use positive language, focus on exciting new experiences, and also acknowledge any fears or concerns.

- **Visitation Days:** If possible, organize a few days where your child can visit the new school or classroom. Familiarizing with the new environment can ease many anxieties.

- **Visual Aids:** Use picture books or social stories that revolve around school transitions. These can serve as gentle introductions to what lies ahead.

Setting Expectations and Routines:

Children, especially those on the autism spectrum, often find comfort in predictability.

- **Consistent Routines:** While some routines might change, like waking up a bit earlier, try to keep the rest of the day's structure consistent, especially during the initial weeks.

- **Mock Days:** Before the school year starts, have a few 'practice' days. Go through the new routine—waking up, getting ready, driving to school, and so on.

- **Visual Schedules:** Use visual schedules to highlight the differences and similarities between the old and new routines. This can serve as a comforting reminder that not everything is changing.

Ensuring Continuity in Support Systems:

Support plays a pivotal role during transitions. Ensure that the safety nets in place continue to provide the comfort they always have.

- **Collaborative Meetings:** Arrange meetings with the new educators, therapists, or support staff. Ensure they're aware of your child's strengths, challenges, and any strategies that have proven effective in the past.

- **Stay Connected:** Just because you're transitioning doesn't mean you need to sever ties with the previous support systems. Sometimes, a familiar face or a quick chat with a previous teacher can provide immense comfort.

- **Feedback Loops:** Keep communication channels open. Regular check-ins with your child, educators, and support staff can ensure that any challenge is addressed promptly.

In essence, transitioning between educational phases is akin to turning the pages of a book. While each chapter brings new adventures, it's all part of the same beautiful story. As caregivers and parents, our role is to ensure that these pages turn smoothly and that every new chapter is approached with hope, excitement, and the reassurance of unwavering support.

Chapter Eight

Family Dynamics

Strengthening Bonds and Understanding

"In family life, love is the oil that eases friction, the cement that binds closer together, and the music that brings harmony." - Friedrich Nietzsche

Navigating the intricate tapestry of family relationships can be both a joy and a challenge. When autism is added to this mix, the dynamics can sometimes become more complex. But with understanding, patience, and a commitment to growth, families can emerge stronger, more connected, and with a deeper appreciation for each other's unique strengths and challenges.

Embracing Every Family Member's Perspective:

Every member of a family experiences the dynamics differently. Parents might grapple with balancing their attention between their children, siblings may sometimes struggle with feelings of being overshadowed or with understanding their autistic sibling's behaviors, and grandparents and extended family members might wrestle with varying levels of awareness and understanding of autism. It's essential to recognize these perspectives and create a space where everyone feels heard, understood, and supported.

Siblings: The Unsung Heroes:

Siblings often play a pivotal role in the life of a child with autism. They can be protectors, companions, mediators, and sometimes even interpreters of the world. But they too need support. It's crucial to acknowledge their feelings, ensure they have their own outlets and safe spaces, and celebrate the unique bond they share with their sibling. Regular one-on-one time, activities that cater to their interests and open channels of communication can work wonders here.

Bonding Activities for the Entire Family:

Introducing activities that cater to every family member's interests and strengths can be a great way to foster unity. These could range from sensory-friendly family outings to board game nights, art and craft sessions, or even quiet reading evenings. The goal is to create memories together, celebrate each individual, and reinforce the idea that every family member brings something valuable to the table.

Open Conversations: The Key to Understanding:

Creating an environment where every family member feels comfortable expressing their feelings, concerns, and joys is paramount. Regular family meetings, open-ended conversations, and even bringing in professionals for guidance can be beneficial. These platforms can be vital in addressing any misconceptions, feelings of guilt or resentment, and in celebrating achievements.

Extended Family and Friends: Building a Supportive Community:

Often, extended family members and friends can play an instrumental role in providing support. Educating them about autism, sharing personal experiences, and including them in the journey can be enlightening for them and beneficial for the immediate family. Organizing family gatherings, workshops, or even informal coffee sessions can help in bridging gaps of understanding.

Seeking External Support:

There's immense strength in seeking support when needed. Whether it's joining a local support group, enrolling in workshops, or seeking counseling, external perspectives can often provide clarity, comfort, and new strategies to strengthen family dynamics.

In the end, every family's journey is unique. But at the core of every journey lies love, resilience, and the unwavering belief that together, as a unit, challenges can be overcome, and joys can be multiplied. With every step, families can move towards a more harmonious, understanding, and connected future.

***

Building Sibling Relationships

In the intricate web of family dynamics, the relationship between siblings holds a special significance. When one sibling has autism, the bond may take on added layers of complexity, but also deeper avenues of connection, growth, and understanding.

Nurturing Understanding and Patience:

Understanding is the foundation stone upon which strong sibling bonds are built. It's essential for siblings to have an understanding of what autism means. Offering age-appropriate books, videos, or discussions can demystify any misconceptions or fears. It's also important to nurture patience. There might be times when the sibling with autism needs more attention or faces challenges. Acknowledging the feelings of the neurotypical sibling and reassuring them of their importance in the family can go a long way in nurturing patience and empathy.

Encouraging Shared Activities and Bonding Time:

Finding common ground is key. This could be in the form of shared hobbies, games, or even simple routines like reading a bedtime story together. For instance, if one child enjoys painting and the other has a fondness for tactile sensations, a joint finger-painting session could be the perfect bonding activity. It's not just about doing things together, but also creating memories, understanding each other's likes and dislikes, and finding joy in shared experiences.

Celebrating the Unique Bond of Siblings:

Every sibling relationship is unique and should be celebrated for its own merits. Siblings may develop their own language, rituals, and inside jokes. They may find solace in each other during challenging times and become each other's biggest cheerleaders during moments of triumph. Regularly acknowledging the importance of this bond, perhaps through special 'sibling days' or memory-making activities, can instill a sense of pride in the relationship.

In conclusion, fostering a harmonious sibling relationship in a family where autism is a part of the equation might require conscious efforts, but the rewards are multifold. It's about building bridges of understanding, creating shared moments, and celebrating the invaluable bond that siblings share, one that lasts a lifetime.

***

Engaging Extended Family

The saying, "It takes a village to raise a child," rings especially true for families touched by autism. Extended family members, from grandparents to uncles, aunts, and cousins, play a pivotal role in the life tapestry of a child with autism. However, engaging in this broader circle requires a harmonious blend of education, boundary-setting, and embracing support.

Educating and Creating Awareness:

Not all extended family members might be familiar with the nuances of autism. It's crucial to bridge this knowledge gap to foster understanding and empathy. Share resources like books, documentaries, or even personal anecdotes that can provide insights into the world of autism. Hosting a family gathering dedicated to understanding and discussing autism can be beneficial. It's not just about sharing challenges but also celebrating the unique gifts and perspectives that autism brings to the table.

Setting Boundaries and Expectations:

Every child, with or without autism, thrives in an environment of consistency. Extended family members should be made aware of specific routines, sensitivities, or triggers. This could be as simple as explaining the child's dietary restrictions or their need for quiet time. But it's equally essential to express gratitude when family members respect these boundaries and help maintain a sense of normalcy for the child. Clear communication is the key, to ensuring that everyone is on the same page, making family gatherings and interactions smoother and more enjoyable for all.

Embracing the Larger Support Network:

Extended family can be an invaluable support network, providing respite for parents, varied interactions for the child, and a sense of continuity and belonging. Organize regular family get-togethers, allowing the child to interact with different family members in varied settings. Embrace the strengths of each family member, be it a grandparent's storytelling prowess or an uncle's knack for music, to enrich the child's experiences.

In the grand symphony of life, the extended family adds richer notes and harmonies. By educating, setting clear expectations, and weaving them into the support fabric, families can ensure that their child with autism feels the warmth, acceptance, and joy of belonging to a larger, loving clan.

***

Carving Out Family Time

In our bustling modern world, the demands of daily life can often make families feel like ships passing in the night. The saying, "Quality over quantity," has never been more pertinent when it comes to spending time with loved ones. Especially for families with a child with autism, carving out dedicated family time is not just beneficial—it's transformative. Here's how you can cultivate those precious moments:

Establishing Routines and Traditions:

Routines offer comfort and predictability to children with autism. While the world outside may be chaotic and ever-changing, having set family routines provides a comforting anchor. This could be something as simple as a Friday night movie, a Sunday morning pancake ritual, or a monthly nature walk. Traditions, too, play a similar role but on a grander scale. Annual camping trips, festive family gatherings, or even birthday rituals become eagerly anticipated events, offering security and a sense of belonging.

Prioritizing Connection and Shared Experiences:

It's not just about being physically present with each other, but truly connecting heart-to-heart. This means putting away distractions, being fully present, and diving into shared activities. Whether it's building a puzzle together, cooking a meal, or just lying on the grass gazing at the stars, it's these shared experiences that deepen bonds. For a child with autism, these moments can be therapeutic, reinforcing their sense of being cherished and valued.

Creating Memories and Building Family Narratives:

Life is a mosaic of memories, and families are the artists that piece them together. Every shared experience, every laughter, even those fleeting quiet moments, become part of your family's unique narrative. Capture these memories—through photos, journals, or even voice recordings. Over time, revisiting these memories becomes a tradition in itself, a beautiful way to reflect on the journey so far and dream about adventures yet to come.

In conclusion, while the world races on, pausing to cherish family time is the oasis every soul craves. For families touched by autism, these moments aren't just about relaxation; they are about reaffirmation—of love, understanding, and the joy of being together.

***

Balancing Needs and Responsibilities

Ah, the ever-evolving dance of family dynamics. Every family member, each with their unique needs and aspirations, comes together under one roof, creating a beautiful, albeit sometimes chaotic, symphony. When you add the unique aspects of autism into this mix, the dynamic can become even more intricate. It's a delicate act, ensuring everyone's needs are met while also holding the family unit harmoniously together. Let's delve into how you can strike that balance:

Recognizing the Diverse Needs of Family Members:

Within a family, there's a broad spectrum of needs. While your child with autism might require a structured routine or sensory accommodations, another member might crave spontaneous family outings or time for solitary reflection. Recognizing these diverse needs is the first step. Open dialogues, regular family check-ins, or even something as simple as a shared family calendar can help ensure everyone's requirements are visible and valued.

Ensuring Self-care and Respite:

This cannot be stressed enough—taking care of yourself is pivotal. As the adage goes, "You can't pour from an empty cup." Especially for primary caregivers, the journey with autism, while incredibly rewarding, can sometimes be exhausting. Finding moments for self-care, be it through meditation, hobbies, or even short breaks, can rejuvenate you. Respite care or seeking support from trusted family or friends can be invaluable. Remember, seeking help isn't a sign of weakness; it's a testament to your strength and understanding of your own needs.

Celebrating Teamwork and Collective Growth:

Families are, in essence, life's first team. Every challenge tackled, and every hurdle overcome, strengthens this team's bonds. Celebrate the small wins, whether it's a new word your child learned, a sibling mastering the art of patience, or you managing to squeeze in some 'me' time. These are all milestones in the family's collective journey. Cherish them, talk about them, and let them serve as reminders of the growth you're achieving together.

In the end, striking a balance is an ongoing process, and perfection isn't the goal. The aim is to cultivate an environment where love reigns supreme, understanding is the cornerstone, and every family member, with their unique needs, feels valued and heard.

***

Crafting a Family Vision

When we think of visions, we often think of companies or organizations setting forth their future aspirations. But just like these entities, families too benefit from having a clear vision. Having a shared direction can serve as a guiding light, helping every member understand their roles, feel valued, and move cohesively towards shared goals. Let's delve into how we can craft this integral vision for our families:

Setting Goals and Aspirations as a Unit:

Every family member, no matter how young or old, has dreams and aspirations. Setting aside time, perhaps during a family dinner or a weekend gathering, to openly discuss these dreams can be enlightening. What does each member hope for in the coming years? Perhaps it's a particular vacation, academic achievement, or simply cultivating certain values. Pooling these dreams together and identifying shared goals can create a unified direction for the family. This becomes especially important in families with autistic members, as understanding their unique aspirations and integrating them into the family vision is essential.

Recognizing and Valuing Individual Contributions:

Every family member brings a unique strength to the table. While one might be the peacemaker, another might excel in organization. Recognizing these strengths and celebrating them is crucial. It's essential to create an atmosphere where everyone feels their contributions, however big or small, are recognized and valued. In the context of autism, this might mean celebrating the small milestones achieved by the autistic family member or acknowledging the patience and understanding of siblings. These recognitions cement the belief that every family member plays an indispensable role in realizing the family's vision.

Nurturing a Safe and Loving Environment for All:

The cornerstone of any family vision should be creating a safe and loving environment. The world outside can sometimes be challenging and unpredictable, especially for those with autism. The family should be a haven where each member, irrespective of their differences, feels unconditionally loved, understood, and safe. This might mean setting certain ground rules, fostering open communication, or dedicating time to shared activities that strengthen bonds.

In crafting this vision, it's important to remember that it isn't a static entity. As family members grow, evolve, and change, the vision too will need revisiting and refining. However, the core essence remains the same: to create a united family front where every member feels valued, understood, and loved.

Chapter Nine

Navigating Challenges and Celebrating Successes

"Every child is a different kind of flower, and all together, they make this world a beautiful garden." - Unknown

Life is a vibrant tapestry of experiences. For every challenge, there's a victory; for every tear, there's a moment of joy. Families, especially those nurturing a member with autism, often find themselves at the crossroads of numerous challenges. Yet, it's the approach toward these challenges and the celebration of small victories that truly define the journey. In this chapter, we delve deep into understanding the essence of navigating the hurdles while keeping the spirit of celebration alive.

Understanding the Nature of Challenges:

Every challenge, whether it's a meltdown in the supermarket or difficulty in comprehending a social situation, has an underlying reason. Often, these challenges arise from the unique way individuals with autism perceive and process the world around them. The first step to navigating these challenges is to understand their origin, to be empathetic, and to approach them without judgment or preconceived notions.

Tools and Techniques for Overcoming Hurdles:

While challenges are inevitable, they aren't insurmountable. There exists a plethora of tools, strategies, and approaches that can assist in managing and, at times, even preventing certain challenges. From visual aids, and structured routines, to therapeutic interventions—there's a tool for every challenge. The key lies in identifying which tool aligns best with the nature of the challenge and the individual's unique needs.

The Power of Positive Reinforcement:

Celebrate, celebrate, celebrate! Every hurdle crossed, every new word spoken, and every social cue understood is a victory. And these victories, no matter how small, deserve celebration. Positive reinforcement, be it through words of encouragement, a favorite treat, or a simple hug, goes a long way in instilling confidence and motivation. It emphasizes the message that efforts are recognized and valued.

Reflecting and Growing Together:

Challenges, while daunting, are also opportunities for growth. They present moments to reflect, learn, and adapt. As a family, it's essential to discuss the challenges faced, to understand what worked and what didn't, and to strategize for the future. This reflective practice not only equips the family to handle similar challenges in the future but also strengthens the bond among members.

Keeping the Spirit High:

The journey of a family with an autistic member is a rollercoaster of emotions. There are highs and lows, laughter and tears. But amidst all this, the spirit of love, understanding, and unity should remain unwavering. Keeping morale high, focusing on the positives, and always being each other's pillar of support is what makes the journey not just worthwhile, but also beautiful.

In conclusion, the challenges faced are but a chapter in the grand story of life. By navigating them with patience, love, and understanding, and by celebrating every success, big or small, families can write a tale filled with warmth, growth, and endless love.

***

Understanding and Managing Meltdowns

One of the most profound and challenging experiences for families nurturing a child with autism is encountering meltdowns. Unlike typical tantrums, meltdowns can be a sensory or emotional overload manifesting physically and emotionally. They can be intense, overwhelming, and often misunderstood. But with understanding and compassion, they can be navigated, and the frequency and intensity can sometimes be reduced.

Recognizing the difference between meltdowns and tantrums:

At first glance, a meltdown might seem like a tantrum, but there are distinct differences. While tantrums often have a purpose, like seeking attention or getting a desired outcome, meltdowns stem from overwhelming feelings or sensory overload. They aren't manipulative or purposeful; they're a genuine reaction to feeling overwhelmed. Often, during a meltdown, the child isn't aware of their surroundings or the people around them, while during a tantrum, there's usually an awareness of the audience.

Example: Imagine two scenarios. In the first, Sarah, a child with autism, is at a bustling supermarket with her mother. The fluorescent lights, humming of fridges, chatter, and the intercom announcement converge into an overwhelming sensory experience for Sarah. She starts to cover her ears, then tears form, and suddenly, she's on the floor, seemingly unaware of the concerned onlookers. This is a meltdown.

In the second scenario, Sarah is at home and wants a cookie before dinner. Her mother says no. Sarah cries and stamps her feet, glancing intermittently at her mom to gauge her reaction. This is a tantrum. While both situations are challenging, understanding the differences helps tailor the response effectively.

Proactive measures to prevent meltdowns:

Prevention, while not always possible, is a vital aspect of managing meltdowns. Observing patterns, recognizing triggers, and intervening before the situation escalates can be effective. This might mean ensuring the child doesn't get too hungry, too tired, or is not exposed to overwhelming stimuli for extended periods. Simple techniques like using visual schedules, giving advance notice of transitions, or having a calm-down kit on hand can make a significant difference.

Example: Over time, Sarah's mom observes that crowded places with loud noises tend to trigger meltdowns. So, they start using noise-cancelling headphones during shopping trips. Additionally, they develop a 'sensory map' of sorts, marking places that have been overwhelming for Sarah in the past. This map helps them plan visits or find quieter times to go to potentially triggering locations.

Compassionate responses during and after a meltdown:

When a meltdown occurs, safety and understanding should be the priority. Ensure the child is in a safe environment where they can't hurt themselves or others. Reduce sensory stimuli, if possible. Speak in a calm, reassuring voice, or sometimes, simply be present without talking. It's crucial to remember that the child is not giving you a hard time; they're having a hard time.

During the Meltdown:

Let's take the supermarket example. Sarah's mother could try the following:

1. **Safety First:** Ensure Sarah is safe and not in a location where she could get hurt, like near a cart or an aisle's edge.

2. **Quiet Corner:** If feasible, move to a quieter aisle or corner of the store where stimuli are reduced.

3. **Reassurance:** Kneel down to Sarah's level, maintaining a calm demeanor, and say softly, "It's okay, Sarah. I'm here with you."

4. **Distraction Tool:** Sarah's mother could keep a favorite soft toy or object in her bag, which she gives to Sarah to focus on.

After the Meltdown:

1. **Reflection without Blame:** Once home and settled, Sarah's mom might say, "I noticed the store was very noisy today. It seemed like it was too much. Would headphones help next time?"

2. **Affirmation:** Reiterate love and understanding. "It's okay to feel overwhelmed sometimes. We'll figure this out together."

3. **Visual Aids:** Use a chart or picture cards to discuss feelings and, if Sarah is receptive, to understand her perspective better.

Remember, every child is unique, and while these examples might work for some, it's essential to tailor strategies to each individual child's needs and experiences.

Post-meltdown, it's beneficial to reflect without assigning blame. Engage in a gentle conversation if the child is willing and able. Reassure them of your love and understanding. Over time, by recognizing patterns and triggers, families can develop strategies tailored to their child's needs, ensuring the child feels safe, understood, and loved.

Empowering Independence and Self-Advocacy

Navigating the world with autism can be a unique journey, laden with challenges but also ripe with opportunities for growth and self-discovery. As caregivers, teachers, or loved ones, our role isn't just to protect and provide—it's also to empower. Let's delve deeper into how we can set the stage for independence and self-advocacy.

Encouraging Age-Appropriate Responsibilities:

Just like every other child, children with autism benefit from being entrusted with responsibilities. It not only cultivates a sense of ownership and pride but also sharpens life skills.

Example: For a young child, this might mean setting the table before dinner or watering plants. As they grow older, responsibilities can evolve into organizing their study table, helping with grocery shopping, or even managing a small weekly allowance. The key is to match the responsibility with their current abilities, providing just the right amount of challenge without overwhelming them.

Teaching Self-Advocacy Skills:

Equip them with tools to understand and communicate their needs, rights, and feelings. This is an invaluable life skill that can have profound implications for their well-being and independence.

Example: Let's say a teen with autism feels overwhelmed by the noise in the school cafeteria. Equipping them with self-advocacy skills might mean they can approach a teacher or staff member to explain their discomfort and possibly ask for an alternative place to eat. Role-playing can be an effective tool here, allowing them to practice such scenarios in a safe environment before they face them in real life.

Celebrating Autonomy and Achievements:

Every step towards independence, no matter how small, deserves recognition. It bolsters confidence and reinforces the idea that they are capable.

Example: Maybe your child managed to complete a task on their own for the first time, like making a sandwich or taking public transport. Celebrate these milestones! It could be with words of affirmation, a special treat, or by simply spending quality time together. Remember, it's not about the magnitude of the achievement but the effort and progress they've made.

As we journey alongside them, it's crucial to remember that every child with autism has their unique strengths, aspirations, and challenges. By fostering a supportive environment that empowers them to thrive on their terms, we set the foundation for a life of confidence, autonomy, and fulfillment.

***

Engaging in Self-Care as a Caregiver

Walking alongside a child with autism is a journey of profound love, patience, and understanding. While the emphasis often falls on the well-being of the child, it's vital not to overlook the well-being of the caregiver. Just like the adage goes, "You cannot pour from an empty cup." Let's delve into the why's and how's of self-care for those who spend their days caring for others.

The Importance of Self-Care for Sustainability:

Your dedication to your loved one is commendable, but sustainability is key. By taking the time for self-care, you recharge and rejuvenate, ensuring you can continue offering the best of yourself. Think of it this way: an artist wouldn't paint with frayed brushes. They maintain their tools to create the best work. In this scenario, you're both the artist and the tool. Regular maintenance – or self-care – ensures your best efforts in caregiving.

Recognizing and Addressing Burnout:

Burnout isn't just a buzzword; it's a real phenomenon that many caregivers experience. Symptoms might include feelings of exhaustion, decreased pleasure in activities you once enjoyed, and even physical ailments. However, acknowledging burnout is the first step in addressing it.

Tip: Maintain a journal. Write down your feelings at the end of the day. This can serve as an outlet and also help you identify patterns or specific triggers leading to burnout. Once identified, you can start to find ways to mitigate them, be it through delegating certain tasks, seeking professional counseling, or merely setting aside quiet time each day.

Creating a Support Network for Yourself:

No matter how resilient or strong-willed you are, everyone needs a village. Your support network can consist of family, friends, fellow caregivers, or professional counselors. These are individuals you can lean on, share experiences with, or simply have a coffee and chat.

Tip: Consider joining a caregiver support group in your community or online. Such groups can be invaluable, offering a space to share, learn, and be heard. You'll often find that your experiences resonate with many others, offering comfort in the shared journey.

In the world of caregiving, it's easy to lose oneself in the myriad of tasks and responsibilities. But remember, taking care of yourself isn't an act of selfishness; it's a necessity. It ensures that you're present, both physically and emotionally, for your loved ones. Celebrate yourself, seek support, and cherish the moments of tranquility and joy. They're not just luxuries; they're integral to your well-being and, by extension, to the well-being of those you care for.

***

Evolving with Your Child's Growth

As the familiar saying goes, the only constant in life is change. Just as seasons change, so too does your child grow, evolve, and transition through various phases of life. As a caregiver, understanding and evolving alongside your child's growth is vital. Let's delve deeper into the nuances of these transitions and how you can best navigate them.

Adapting Techniques for Different Developmental Stages:

From the bubbling energy of toddlerhood to the growing independence of the preteen years, each developmental phase comes with its set of joys and challenges. What worked wonders for your three-year-old might not be as effective for your eight-year-old.

Example: When teaching communication skills to a toddler, visual aids and physical prompts might be essential. However, as they progress to school-age, role-playing or using stories can be more impactful. It's all about aligning your strategies with their current developmental needs.

Preparing for and Navigating Puberty with Autism:

Puberty is a tumultuous period for any individual, with a whirlwind of physical, emotional, and social changes. For a child with autism, these transitions can feel even more magnified.

Example: Sensory sensitivities might increase with the onset of puberty. You might notice a teenager with autism becoming more agitated by clothing textures or certain sounds. In these situations, providing them with sensory tools or creating a sensory-friendly environment becomes paramount. Additionally, using social stories can be an effective method to introduce them to the changes their body will undergo, ensuring they don't feel overwhelmed or surprised.

Transitioning to Adulthood and Beyond:

Entering adulthood is a significant milestone. It's a phase marked by a search for independence, identity, and purpose.

Example: Vocational training can be introduced to young adults with autism to help them find a potential career path or passion. Furthermore, life skills such as budgeting, cooking, and navigating public transportation can be taught to promote independence. As for emotional growth, continuing to foster open communication ensures that they always have a safe space to share their feelings, concerns, and aspirations.

Life is an ever-evolving journey, and the path of raising a child with autism is no different. While each phase brings its set of challenges, it also offers countless moments of joy, growth, and bonding. Embrace each stage, arm yourself with knowledge and strategies, and remember that every transition is an opportunity for both you and your child to learn, grow, and flourish together.

***

Cherishing the Journey and Celebrating Milestones

It's often said that life is not about the destination, but the journey. When walking alongside a loved one with autism, this sentiment resonates profoundly. The path might be strewn with challenges, but it's also illuminated with moments of sheer joy, growth, and deep connection.

Reflecting on the Growth and Progress:

The days might seem long, but years are short. Amidst the daily routines, therapies, and strategies, it's easy to lose sight of how far you and your child have come. Taking moments to pause and reflect can offer much-needed perspective. Remember that day when tying shoelaces felt impossible, or when a simple trip to the grocery store seemed overwhelming? Look at where you are now! It's essential to reminisce about these moments, not just to appreciate the growth but also to understand that every challenge faced has shaped this beautiful journey.

Recognizing and Celebrating Small Wins:

In the intricate dance of growth, it's not just the giant leaps that matter but also the tiny, seemingly inconsequential steps. The first time your child tries a new food without a fuss, when they manage to express a complex emotion or even when they bravely face a previously daunting sensory challenge – these are all victories, deserving of celebration. These moments, however small they might seem, are foundational in building confidence and resilience.

Example: Create a "Victory Jar" at home. Every time your child (or even you) achieves something, no matter how trivial it seems, write it down on a slip of paper and pop it into this jar. On particularly challenging days, or at the end of the year, open this jar and read through the victories. It serves as a heartwarming reminder of the strength, progress, and countless happy moments.

Envisioning a Bright and Promising Future:

With every challenge surmounted and every milestone achieved, the horizon only gets brighter. It's crucial to maintain an optimistic outlook. While there will always be hurdles, there's also an abundance of potential waiting to be unlocked. Dream big for your child. Allow them to dream too, and always keep those dreams alive. The possibilities are endless.

Your journey with your child is a tapestry woven with threads of resilience, growth, challenges, and countless celebrations. Cherish every moment, every memory, and every milestone. Here's to the journey, the lessons, and the love that keeps propelling us forward.

Chapter Ten

Conclusion

Celebrating Uniqueness and Embracing the Journey

As we draw this guide to a close, I'd like to take a moment to applaud you, dear reader. Your dedication, your unwavering love, and your ceaseless efforts in understanding and supporting your loved one with autism are genuinely commendable. The pages we've navigated together have offered strategies, insights, and stories, but the real essence of this journey lies in the heartbeats between these lines – in the laughter, the tears, the triumphs, and the challenges.

Every child is a universe unto themselves, brimming with potential and promise. Autism, with its unique tapestry of experiences, brings forth a kaleidoscope of emotions, learnings, and moments that are both challenging and rewarding. It's a journey of discovery – about your child, about autism, but also about yourself. Through the highs and lows, remember that every challenge faced is also an opportunity for growth.

In your quest to provide the best for your loved one, remember to also be kind to yourself. The road might sometimes feel overwhelming, but you're never truly alone. Lean on your support systems, cherish the community around you, and always, always hold onto hope.

While strategies and techniques are essential, the heart of the matter is the connection, understanding, and unconditional love. Celebrate the milestones, no matter how small. Rejoice in the uniqueness of your child. And above all, embrace the beautiful, unpredictable journey that lies ahead.

Thank you for allowing me to be a part of your journey. Here's to a future filled with understanding, joy, growth, and countless moments of love and connection.